History of American Higher Education

PRIMER

PETER LANG
New York • Washington, D.C./Baltimore • Bern
Frankfurt • Berlin • Brussels • Vienna • Oxford

Margaret Cain McCarthy

History of American Higher Education
PRIMER

PETER LANG
New York • Washington, D.C./Baltimore • Bern
Frankfurt • Berlin • Brussels • Vienna • Oxford

Library of Congress Cataloging-in-Publication Data

McCarthy, Margaret Cain.
History of American higher education primer /
Margaret Cain McCarthy.
p. cm. — (Peter Lang primers)
Includes bibliographical references and index.
1. Education, Higher—United States—History.
2. Universities and colleges—United States—History.
I. Title.
LA226.M135   378.73—dc22   2011002741
ISBN 978-1-4331-1165-5

Bibliographic information published by **Die Deutsche Nationalbibliothek**.
Die Deutsche Nationalbibliothek lists this publication in the "Deutsche
Nationalbibliografie"; detailed bibliographic data is available
on the Internet at http://dnb.d-nb.de/.

FSC
Mixed Sources
Product group from well-managed
forests, controlled sources and
recycled wood or fiber

Cert no. SCS-COC-002464
www.fsc.org
©1996 Forest Stewardship Council

Cover design by Clear Point Designs

The paper in this book meets the guidelines for permanence and durability
of the Committee on Production Guidelines for Book Longevity
of the Council of Library Resources.

© 2011 Peter Lang Publishing, Inc., New York
29 Broadway, 18th floor, New York, NY 10006
www.peterlang.com

Printed in the United States of America

Contents

1: Overview of Higher Education in the United States   1
    Introduction   1
    Number and Types of Institutions   2
    Faculty   6
    Students   6
    Alumni   8
    Conclusion   9

2: Colonial and Early American Colleges, 1636–1800   11
    Foundation   11
    Structure and Governance   17
    Tutors/Faculty and Curriculum   19
    Students and Student Life   24

3: Growth and Change, 1800–1900   27
    The New Century   27
    Public/Private Distinction: The Dartmouth College Case 30
    Trustees of Dartmouth College v. Woodward, 17 U.S.
        (4 Wheat.) 518 (1819)   35
    The Yale Report of 1828   38
    Institutional Diversification   39

Women's Colleges 40
Historically Black Colleges and Universities 45
Normal Schools 48
Professional Education 50
Catholic Colleges and Universities 52
State Universities 56
Research Universities, Graduate Institutions,
 and Technical Schools 58
Land-Grant Colleges 61
Faculty and Governance 63
Student Life 66

4: Expansion of Higher Education, 1900–1960 71
Introduction 71
Evolution of Established Institutions 72
Junior and Community Colleges: Vocational Education 81
Standardization 84
Accreditation and Professional Associations 84
National Collegiate Athletic Association (NCAA) 90
Purpose and Policy: Federal Impact 94
Report of the President's Commission
 on Higher Education, 1947 97
National Defense Education Act (NDEA) of 1958 102
Faculty and Administration 104
Academic Freedom 104
Administration 110
Student Life 112
Student Life and Demographics 112
Standardized Testing 114

5: Access and Choice, 1960–the 21st Century 117
Introduction 117
Higher Education Access and Choice:
Expanding the Federal Role 119
The Higher Education Act of 1965 120
No Child Left Behind Act of 2001 124
A Test of Leadership: Charting the Future
 of U.S. Higher Education (2006) 124
Financing Higher Education 129
Faculty Roles and Challenges 131
Student Life 133

Student Protest   133
Student Enrollment   139
Conclusion   141

6: References and Resources   145
References   145
Additional Resources   152
Relevant Web Sites   154

Complete Glossary   157

Index   161

Overview of Higher Education in the United States

Introduction

American higher education in the 21st century is complex and diverse. Encompassing all varieties of educational opportunity beyond the secondary level, it includes public and private institutions that award certificates, diplomas, or degrees. Some are proprietary schools, operating for a profit and designed to prepare individuals for a specific career. Other institutions focus on the liberal arts and many of them offer both bachelor's and master's degree programs. True universities tend to have a strong research orientation. Admission and graduation requirements vary; expectations for faculty work and productivity differ, as do institutional commitments to community involvement and service. The system of higher education evident in the United States today emerged over a period of more than 370 years. In very general terms, higher education remained relatively consistent in the 1600s and early 1700s but began to diversify after the American Revolution. Throughout the 1800s, the system expanded significantly in an effort to address the needs of a rapidly developing nation. Still, the impact was limited by the narrow influence, modest number, and small size of most institutions. By the end of the 1800s, the

idea that new knowledge could be discovered which could improve the human condition gained prominence. States became college benefactors; public and privately endowed research universities were founded; and land-grant institutions were established through federal legislation. New populations of students enrolled in a variety of academic programs, some of which were intended to support advancement while others were designed to mold students for the established role and place social custom dictated. Throughout the 20th century, the value of a college degree became apparent as an avenue for both social mobility and economic prosperity. Private and government investment, the advent of college athletics, and the development of a knowledge industry combined to amplify the role and raise the value of postsecondary education. The 21st century promises to impact higher education in new ways that will stretch the boundaries of teaching, learning, research, and service as knowledge expands at a seemingly boundless pace and technology pressures **pedagogy** in ways never before imagined.

Pedagogy
instructional methods used in teaching

Number and Types of Institutions

Before focusing on the historical development of higher education in the United States, it is useful to gain an understanding of its 21st-century organizational structure. One way to do so is to view postsecondary education through the classification system developed by the **Carnegie Foundation for the Advancement of Teaching**. First outlined in 1970 and published in 1973, the classifications have been revised and updated several times. The current form offers "multiple, parallel classifications" to allow researchers more flexibility and to offer different "lenses" through which to view and understand higher education (Carnegie Foundation, n.d., "Carnegie Classification," paras. 1-2). The most recent iteration, using data from 2003 and 2004, was published in 2005 and reported 4,391 institutions enrolling over 17.5 million students. Data from Table 1.1 indicate that institutions which primarily offered an **associate's degree** accounted for over 41.4% of all institutions of higher education in the United States and enrolled 39% of all students during the years under review. Of the 1,078 colleges in this category, more than half were **for-profit**. Two hundred eighty-three **research institutions** (6.4% of all) enrolled more

Carnegie Foundation for the Advancement of Teaching
founded by Andrew Carnegie in 1905 and serves as a policy and research center

Associate's degree
academic degree usually awarded after two years of study or the equivalent

For-profit
institutions that operate in order to generate a profit

Research institutions
institutions that conduct research as a primary mission

Table 1.1: 2005 Carnegie Classification of Institutions of Higher Education

	Number of institutions				Share of total number	Total enroll-ment	Share of total enroll-ment
	Public	Private non-profit	For-profit	Total			
Associate colleges							
Public rural-serving small	142	0	0	142	3.2%	133,027	0.8%
Public rural-serving medium	311	0	0	311	7.1%	943,701	5.4%
Public rural-serving large	143	0	0	143	3.3%	1,065,099	6.1%
Public suburban-serving single campus	110	0	0	110	2.5%	854,259	4.9%
Public suburban-serving multicampus	100	0	0	100	2.3%	1,051,012	6.0%
Public urban-serving single campus	32	0	0	32	0.7%	275,307	1.6%
Public urban-serving multi-campus	153	0	0	153	3.5%	1,765,870	10.1%
Public special use	14	0	0	14	0.3%	30,220	0.2%
Private nonprofit	0	114	0	114	2.6%	43,961	0.3%
Private for-profit	0	0	531	531	12.1%	272,833	1.6%
Public 2-year under 4-year universities	55	0	0	55	1.3%	134,222	0.8%
Public 4-year primarily associate	18	0	0	18	0.4%	148,416	0.8%
Private nonprofit 4-year primarily associate	0	20	0	20	0.5%	12,052	0.1%
Private for-profit 4-year primarily associate	0	0	71	71	1.6%	48,272	0.3%
Research institutions							
Research universities very high research activity	63	33	0	96	2.2%	2,365,228	13.5%
Research universities high research activity	76	27	0	103	2.3%	1,693,731	9.6%
Doctoral/research universities	28	48	8	84	1.9%	862,687	4.9%
Master's colleges and universities							
Larger programs	166	161	18	345	7.9%	2,798,279	15.9%
Medium programs	69	108	13	190	4.3%	739,648	4.2%

(Table continued on next page)

(Table continued from previous page)

	Number of institutions						Share of total enroll-ment
	Public	Private non-profit	For-profit	Total	Share of total number	Total enroll-ment	
Smaller programs	32	83	13	128	2.9%	349,859	2.0%
Baccalaureate colleges							
Arts and sciences	38	247	2	287	6.5%	527,533	3.0%
Diverse fields	80	263	17	360	8.2%	595,754	3.4%
Baccalaureate/associate colleges	34	31	55	120	2.7%	267,832	1.5%
Special-focus institutions							
Faith related	0	314	0	314	7.2%	101,742	0.6%
Medical schools and medi-cal centers	29	28	0	57	1.3%	90,701	0.5%
Other health professions	5	99	25	129	2.9%	59,634	0.3%
Engineering	1	5	2	8	0.2%	14,259	0.1%
Other technology	1	6	50	57	1.3%	40,160	0.2%
Business and management	0	25	39	64	1.5%	92,222	0.5%
Art/music/design	4	60	42	106	2.4%	128,273	0.7%
Law	5	25	2	32	0.7%	25,683	0.1%
Other	0	32	7	39	0.9%	17,796	0.1%
Tribal colleges	23	9	0	32	0.7%	17,599	0.1%
Not classified	5	7	14	26	0.6%	3,698	-
All institutions	1,737	1,745	909	4,391	100%	17,570,569	100%

Note: This shows the basic Carnegie classification, a time-specific snapshot of institutional attributes based on data from 2002–2003 and 2003–2004. Institutions might be classified differently using a different time frame. The table reflects corrections of data that had been erroneously reported to the Carnegie Foundation. See http://www.carnegie foundation.org for more information. A dash indicates less than 0.1 percent.

Source: Carnegie Foundation for the Advancement of Teaching

Master's level institutions
institutions that offer a baccalaureate and some master's degree programs

than 4.9 million students, or 28% of all students. Of these research institutions, almost 60% were public. In total, the 663 **master's level institutions** comprised about 15% of all institutions and enrolled about 22% of all students. The majority (53%) of master's colleges and universities were private, nonprofit institutions. Institutions classified

Table 1.2: Degrees Awarded by Type of Institution, 2006–2007

Type of institution	Associate		Bachelor's		Master's		Doctorate		Professional	
	Number	Share of total	Number	Share of total	Number	Share of total	Number	Share of total	Number	Share of total
Public	566,539	78%	975,513	64%	291,971	48%	36,230	60%	36,855	41%
Private nonprofit	43,829	6%	477,805	31%	261,700	43%	22,483	37%	52,746	59%
Private for-profit	117,750	16%	70,774	5%	50,936	8%	1,903	3%	463	1%
All	728,118	100%	1,524,092	100%	604,607	100%	60,616	100%	90,064	100%

Note: Because of rounding, figures may not add up to 100 percent.

Source: U.S. Department of Education

Copyright 2010 *The Chronicle of Higher Education.* Reprinted with permission.

Baccalaureate
academic degree usually
associated with a four-year
undergraduate course of
study

as **baccalaureate** accounted for 17.4% of all institutions but enrolled only 7.9% of all students. Institutions with a special focus enrolled 3.2% of all students at 864 institutions (19.7% of all). The largest of these were faith related, medical schools/centers, and those that concentrated on art, music, and design.

The largest campus-based institution is Miami Dade College in Florida but the trend toward online education is growing. In fall 2007, the University of Phoenix online campus, with 224,880 students, had the largest enrollment of any institution in the nation (U.S. Department of Education, n.d., "Which Colleges Have").

Another way to look at higher education in the United States is to consider degree production. Information in Table 1.2 indicates that in 2006–2007, public institutions awarded the largest share of associate's degrees (78%); the largest share of bachelor's degrees (64%); the largest share of master's degrees (48%); and the largest share of doctorates (60%). However, private nonprofit institutions were a close second at the master's level (43%) and outpaced public institutions at the professional level with 59% of

the total awarded. Private for-profit institutions awarded significantly more associate's degrees (117,118) than degrees at any other level.

Faculty

Historical patterns of educational opportunity and achievement are reflected in the composition of faculty today. As data in Table 1.3 indicate, men account for 127,488 (74%) of the faculty at the highest rank, full professor. Women account for only 45,907 (26%) of full professors but are making steady advances at the ranks of associate professor, where they account for 40% of the total, and assistant professor, where they comprise 47% of the total. Overall, the vast majority (77%) are White.

Students

The U.S. Census Bureau reported approximately 17.8 million individuals age 14 years and older enrolled in college in 2007. The majority were women, accounting for over 10 million of the total. During the past twenty years, the number of students over 25 years of age has increased and more come from diverse backgrounds yet the majority of college students are in the 18- to 24-year-old range (63%) and the majority (77%) are White. There were 2.47 million Black students and 2.13 million students of Hispanic origin enrolled in 2007, in both cases continuing a trend toward higher levels of enrollment (U.S. Census Bureau, 2010, #272). The number of international students studying in the United States has grown significantly. In 1990, there were approximately 391,500 international students and in 2008 there were 624,500, an increase of about 60% (U.S. Census Bureau, 2010, #270).

Data from the U.S. Census Bureau for 2007 indicate that of the 1,524,092 bachelor's degrees awarded, the greatest number were conferred in business (327,531) followed by social sciences and history (164,183); education (105,641); and health professions and related sciences (101,810) (U.S. Census Bureau, 2010, #291). At the master's level, the greatest number were awarded in the fields of education (176,572) and business (150,211). At the doctoral level, 60,616 degrees were awarded and the following fields were most popular: health professions and related clinical sciences (8,355); education (8,261); engineering (8,123); bio-

Table 1.3: Number of Full-Time Faculty Members by Sex, Rank, and Racial and Ethnic Group, Fall 2007

	Total	American Indian	Asian	Black	Hispanic	White	Race unknown	Nonresident foreign
Rank								
Professor								
All	173,395	528	12,239	5,839	4,128	147,867	1,309	1,485
Men	127,488	344	10,018	3,646	2,874	108,404	973	1,229
Women	45,907	184	2,221	2,193	1,254	39,463	336	256
Associate professor								
All	143,692	604	11,082	7,855	4,714	115,274	1,628	2,535
Men	86,660	312	7,570	4,110	2,768	68,982	1,038	1,880
Women	57,032	292	3,512	3,745	1,946	46,292	590	655
Assistant professor								
All	168,508	679	17,290	10,642	6,329	117,618	3,593	12,357
Men	88,741	298	10,037	4,607	3,265	60,407	1,945	8,182
Women	79,767	381	7,253	6,035	3,064	57,211	1,648	4,175
Instructor								
All	101,429	965	5,225	7,480	5,800	77,609	2,350	2,000
Men	46,599	492	2,463	2,928	2,782	35,795	1,066	1,073
Women	54,830	473	2,762	4,552	3,018	41,814	1,284	927
Lecturer								
All	31,264	151	2,081	1,602	1,492	23,470	661	1,807
Men	14,784	77	956	721	613	11,045	347	1,025
Women	16,480	74	1,125	881	879	12,425	314	782
Other								
All	85,175	413	5,744	4,512	2,512	58,622	2,334	11,038
Men	44,843	196	3,134	1,770	1,166	29,742	1,291	7,544
Women	40,332	217	2,610	2,742	1,346	28,880	1,043	3,494
Total								
All	703,463	3,340	53,661	37,930	24,975	540,460	11,875	31,222
Men	409,115	1,719	34,178	17,782	13,468	314,375	6,660	20,933
Women	294,348	1,621	19,483	20,148	11,507	226,085	5,215	10,289

Note: Totals may differ from figures reported in other tables because of varying survey methodologies. Source: U.S. Department of Education

logical and biomedical sciences (6,354); psychology (5,153); and physical sciences (4,846) (U.S. Census Bureau, 2010, #292).

The average annual cost for undergraduate tuition and room and board in 2007–08 was estimated to be $11,578 at public institutions and $29,915 at private institutions. In the ten-year period between 1997–98 and 2007–08, these costs rose about 30% at public institutions and 23% at private institutions, after adjusting for inflation (U.S. Department of Education, National Center for Education Statistics, n.d., Table 331). At the undergraduate level in 2007–08, 66% of all students received some type of financial aid. The total average (for those who received aid) was $9,100. Fifty-two percent received grants averaging $4,900, and 38% took out an average of $7,100 in student loans. Seven percent received aid through work-study jobs (averaging $2,400 in wages) and 2% received an average of $5,400 in veterans' benefits. Four percent of students had parents who took out an average of $10,800 in Parent PLUS loans (Wei, Berkner, He, Lew, Cominole, & Siegel, 2009, p. 3).

Alumni

The purpose and value of higher education has been much debated over the years. Some argue that knowledge is valuable in and of itself. Critical thinking and communication skills often credited to higher education are also understood by many to be important qualities for a full and productive life. Others cite increased earning power as an important purpose of higher education. In 2008, the percentage of young adults working full-time for the full year was generally higher for those with higher levels of education. Seventy-two percent of young adults with a bachelor's degree or higher were full-time, full-year workers in 2008, compared with 62% of young adults with a high school diploma or its equivalent. Among young adults employed full-time, full-year, higher levels of education were associated with higher median earnings. This pattern of higher earnings corresponding with higher levels of educational attainment was consistent for each year between 1995 and 2008. Young adults with a bachelor's degree consistently had higher median earnings than those with less education, and this pattern held for male, female, White, Black,

Hispanic, and Asian subgroups. According to the National Center for Education Statistics in 2008:

> The median of the earnings of young adults with a bachelor's degree was $46,000, while the median was $36,000 for those with an associate's degree, $30,000 for those with a high school diploma or its equivalent, and $23,500 for those who did not earn a high school diploma or its equivalent. In other words, in 2008, young adults with a bachelor's degree earned 28 percent more than young adults with an associate's degree, 53 percent more than young adult high school completers, and 96 percent more than young adults who did not earn a high school diploma. In 2008, the median of the earnings of young adults with a master's degree or higher was $55,000—20 percent more than young adults with a bachelor's degree. (U.S. Department of Education, National Center for Education Statistics, n.d., "What Is the Average Income")

Institutional alumni who remember their college years fondly or credit their earning potential to their *alma mater* also donate to their former institutions. As a result of their generosity and that of other interested individuals and organizations, institutional endowments have grown at some institutions to astounding levels. The nation's first college, Harvard, reported its endowment in 2009 to be over $25 billion. Yale University, Stanford University, and Princeton University each reported endowments that year of over $10 billion (NACUBO and Commonfund Institute, 2010). In 2009, voluntary support for higher education exceeded $28 billion, the largest percentage of which came from foundations (29.6%), followed by alumni (25.6%), non-alumni individuals (17.9%), and corporations (16.6%); religious and other organizations made up the balance (Council for Aid to Education, 2009, p. 2).

Conclusion

Postsecondary education in the United States has developed in response to social expectations, economic opportunities, political agendas, global pressures, and national needs. Still, the experience of higher education remains an individual one, reflecting the goals, aspirations, and hopes of individual students throughout its history. While critics might complain that the system is slow to change, others cite its rapid expansion, especially during the 20th century, as evidence of its vitality. The broad overview offered in this primer reflects the historical progression through which

the system of higher education in the United States developed. It is impossible here to fully describe the complexity of this evolution, the numerous individual visionaries, the countless intertwining details, the sidesteps, and the missteps that all contributed to the size and scope of the contemporary enterprise. Although the development is presented as a linear narrative, it is important to understand that no single institution, or even institutional type, arrived at one particular moment in its current form. The faculty of the classical curriculum often thrived side by side with those who were conducting pure or applied research and others who prepared students for the professions. The interested reader is encouraged to review the reference section and seek out additional material, both on general educational history and on details relative to specific institutions, individuals, and movements.

GLOSSARY

Pedagogy: instructional methods used in teaching

Carnegie Foundation for the Advancement of Teaching: founded by Andrew Carnegie in 1905 and serves as a policy and research center

Associate's degree: academic degree usually awarded after two years of study or the equivalent

For-profit: institutions that operate in order to generate a profit

Research institutions: institutions that conduct research as a primary mission

Master's level institutions: institutions that offer a baccalaureate and some master's degree programs

Baccalaureate: academic degree usually associated with a four-year undergraduate course of study

CHAPTER TWO

Colonial and Early American Colleges, 1636–1800

Foundation

New England
Northeast area of the United States; includes Maine, Vermont, Massachusetts, New Hampshire, Connecticut, and Rhode Island

Puritans
Christian religious group that left England seeking religious freedom

Colonial colleges
nine colleges founded during the colonial period

In 1636, less than ten years after the colony of **New England** was settled, the **Puritans** established Harvard College in order to ensure a civilized society with knowledgeable leaders and an educated clergy. They came to the New World to guarantee their own freedom of religious expression and required leaders who understood the faith and could effectively transmit it to others. Named as a memorial to its benefactor, the Reverend John Harvard, and patterned after Emmanuel College in England, the institution became the first of a very diverse set of institutions of higher education in the United States. The **colonial colleges** that followed Harvard were established with similar goals in mind. In total, nine institutions of higher learning were founded in the American colonies:

1636: Harvard College was founded in Cambridge, Massachusetts, by the Puritans, who were highly educated and determined to establish a successful English colony. The Statutes of Harvard outlined the admission requirements and the expectations of all students. The primary religious mission was clear: "Every one shall consider the

main End of his life and studies, to know God and Jesus Christ which is eternal life. John 17.3." Each student was required to read the scriptures twice a day, attend all classes and lectures, avoid profanity, honor his "parents, Magistrates, Elders, tutors, and aged persons," mind his own affairs, obey the college rules, avoid immoral company, and resist leaving town without the permission of his tutor, parents, or guardians (Statutes of Harvard, 1646, p. 125). Standing as the oldest corporation in the United States, its governance structure established a model still in use today (Thelin, 2004, pp. 1, 11). In order to be successful at Harvard in the 17th century, a student needed some fluency in Latin and at least a basic knowledge of Greek grammar. Three academic exercises, the lecture, the declamation, and the **disputation**, provided the framework for this education. The lecture was designed to teach the students to think logically and systematically. The master would offer a proposition as a question and then proceed to divide the proposition into its various fundamental components, considering the relationships and implications of each. The declamation was a similar student-led exercise that emphasized rhetorical skills. The disputation required a student to respond to a question posed by a moderator and then to answer the objections raised by one or more student respondents. Success required knowledge, wit, and rhetorical skills, all of which were essential to men in leadership positions, whether they be clergy, government officers, or businessmen (Cremin, 1970, pp. 45–46).

Disputation
formalized method of debate

1693: The College of William and Mary was founded in Williamsburg, Virginia, by the Anglicans. Professors were required to be Anglican and the college president was the head of the church in Virginia. Several of the colonial colleges, including Harvard and William and Mary, established Indian schools in an effort to Christianize the native population. The Royal Charter for William and Mary noted as one of the college's missions "that the Christian faith may be propagated amongst the Western Indians, to the glory of Almighty God." With financial support from the estate of Sir Robert Boyle, the college kept "soe many Indian children in Sicknesse and health, in Meat, drink, Washing, Lodgeing, Cloathes, Medicine, books and Education from the first beginning of Letters till they are ready to receive Orders and be thought Sufficient to be

sent abroad to preach and Convert the Indians" (William & Mary, n.d., para. 3).

1701: Yale College (formerly known as the Collegiate School of Connecticut) was founded by the Congregationalists, a group who had split from the Puritans, in part because of Harvard's spirit of **toleration**. Yale professed to be an institution where the faith of the fathers was carefully protected. Very conservative in its early period, toleration was not acceptable until about 1765. Not unlike Harvard, the religious mission of Yale was paramount. In the early 1700s, the primary goal of the institution was that "every student shall consider the main end of his study to wit to knoe God in Jesus Christ and answerably to lead a Godly, sober life" (Ringenberg, 1984, p. 38). In 1718, the Collegiate School was renamed in honor of Elihu Yale in gratitude for his donation of books and goods (Yale University, n.d., para. 2).

Toleration

willingness to allow various Protestant religious denominations

1746: Princeton College (formerly the College of New Jersey) was founded by New Light Presbyterians. The "New Lights" were a product of the **Great Awakening** religious movement around the 1730s. The college moved to its current location in Princeton, New Jersey, in 1756, and in 1896, the College of New Jersey changed its name to Princeton University. Woodrow Wilson, the thirteenth president of the United States, was a Princeton faculty member and served as its president from 1902 to 1910 (Princeton University, n.d., para. 3).

Great Awakening

religious movement around the 1730s

1754: Columbia University (formerly known as King's College) was founded in New York City by the Anglicans. However, in the spirit of toleration, the college charter provided for the election of clergy from four rival Protestant denominations to the board of governors (Rudolph, 1962, p. 16). The eight students who entered the first class in July 1754 were offered an education that was intended to "enlarge the Mind, improve the understanding, polish the whole Man, and qualify them to support the brightest Characters in all the elevated stations in life." Like other colonial colleges, education was suspended as a result of the American Revolution (1775–1783). The college reopened, as Columbia, in 1784. In 1857, the college moved from Park Place to 49th Street and Madison Avenue, where it remained for forty years before moving to its Morningside

Heights campus in 1897 (Columbia University, n.d., paras. 5, 6).

1755: The University of Pennsylvania (originally known as the College and Academy of Philadelphia) was the only one of the early colonial colleges that was not officially church related, although the chief executive officer was Anglican. Under the leadership of Scottish-born William Smith, a three-year course of study was established that was the first in America not derived from medieval tradition and not created for a religious purpose (Rudolph, 1962, pp. 16, 32). The University of Pennsylvania credits Benjamin Franklin as the visionary for the institution which began as an academy and charity school. The school he envisioned would teach both the arts and the practical skills necessary for employment. He advocated for his vision in a pamphlet titled *Proposals for the Education of Youth in Pennsylvania,* assembled the board of trustees, secured a building, and opened his academy in January 1751. The success of the academy led Franklin and the trustees to secure a charter for the College of Philadelphia, which was granted in 1755. The first provost, the Reverend William Smith, designed a curriculum that included the classics and the more practical sciences (McConaghy, Silberman, & Kalashnikova, 2004, paras. 2–5).

1764: Brown University (formerly the College of Rhode Island) was founded by the Baptists but the institution immediately welcomed students from all religious backgrounds. Originally founded as the College of Rhode Island in Warren, Rhode Island, the institution moved to its current location in Providence in 1770. The name changed in 1804 to Brown University in recognition of its benefactor, Nicholas Brown. Women were first admitted to Brown in 1891 through the Women's College, later known as Pembroke College. Following eighty years of this coordinate structure, the Women's College merged with Brown in 1971 (Brown University, n.d., paras. 1–3).

1766: Rutgers (formerly known as Queens College) was founded in New Brunswick, New Jersey, by the Dutch Reformed Church. Opening shortly before the Revolution, the institution faced a difficult transition from colonial to American college. During the war, classes were held sporadically in schools or churches. After the war, still trying

to build a foundation, the college opened and closed several times before establishing itself as Rutgers College, in honor of Colonel Henry Rutgers, a highly regarded member of the Dutch Reformed Church and a veteran of the Revolutionary War (Rutgers University, n.d., paras. 1–3).

1769: Dartmouth College was founded in Hanover, New Hampshire, by the Reverend Eleazar Wheelock, a Congregational minister. He relocated the educational institution he originally established in Lebanon, Connecticut, to Hanover with the assistance of the royal governor of New Hampshire, who provided the land. The institution is named for William Legge, the second Earl of Dartmouth, England (Dartmouth University, n.d., para. 11).

The distinction between public and private colleges was not recognized during the colonial period. Colonial governments often supported the colleges financially and public officials served on their boards yet the institutions were not directly under government control. Often founded by a community's dominant Protestant religious sect, colonial colleges were important to the viability of the community and it was not uncommon for towns to fight over the acquisition or placement of a college. All received some form of financial support from the local government, usually in the form of a grant of land and revenue from one or more taxes. John R. Thelin (2004) argues that "religion occupied a central but confined place in the colonial colleges," and that although the New World offered religious opportunities not available in Europe, that did not necessarily mean the colonies were in favor of religious tolerance. As a result, in the 17th and early 18th centuries, each colony and its college supported, and were supported by, a particular Protestant denomination. By the mid-18th century, some of the newer colleges sought to allow some diversity and balance the representation of denominations on the board in order to keep any single group from gaining full authority (pp. 13–14).

In addition to government subsidies, colleges benefited from the donations of benefactors. The names of (Elihu) Yale and (John) Harvard are easily recognized for their gifts to their namesake institutions. Less well known are the numerous philanthropists in England who were engaged to support the missionary work of the colleges among the American natives. Efforts to transform native people into

English scholars and ministers were not highly successful and, while there is no doubt some of these efforts were sincere, there is also reason to question the depth of commitment of the colonists to this effort. The college curriculum had a strong religious foundation so, in order to be successful, the Indians would have had to dismiss their own beliefs and adopt Christianity. There was little for them to gain in terms of social status or acceptance into colonial culture. Consider that one of the primary purposes of education is the passing on of a civilization's cultural heritage. Clearly, the European heritage had no meaning to the native people, and opportunities for them to fit in to established colonial society, with or without an education, were very limited.

However, proclaimed efforts to Christianize native people did provide a successful platform for fund-raising for several colonial colleges. Scholar Bobby Wright's (1988) examination provides three compelling examples: Harvard, the College of William and Mary, and Dartmouth College. Harvard was established with no professed commitment to native education. However, in 1649 the English Parliament created the Society for the Propagation of the Gospel in New England, the purpose of which was to raise money for native conversion. Shortly after, in 1650, Harvard president Henry Dunster developed the college charter in which he noted that the college provided for "the education of the English and Indian youth of this Country in knowledge: and godliness" (Harvard Charter of 1650, para. 1). Harvard was in need of financial support and, in 1653, the society gave Harvard funds to build an Indian college. The building was twice as large and cost about four times as much as originally proposed. It appears that it was not until 1660 that any native student attended Harvard for a bachelor's degree and never more than two were enrolled. In forty years, only four native students attended, although the building was well used by colonial scholars (Wright, 1988).

James Blair, commissary of Virginia, was successful at procuring funds for the College of William and Mary from the estate of Robert Boyle, governor of the New England Company, on the promise of an Indian school at the prospective new college in Virginia. He obtained a charter for the college in 1693 that included provision for a school to spread the Christian faith among the Indians. There is

no record of native students at the college before 1705. As president of the college, Blair did not seriously attempt to fulfill the wishes of the Boyle estate. Instead, he found various other purposes for the growing fund, including a construction project and library development (Wright, 1988).

Eleazar Wheelock of Dartmouth College was, perhaps, the most successful at raising funds for proposed Indian education. In 1754, he founded Moor's Charity School for Indian students and it operated successfully for nearly a century. In 1763, Wheelock sent a proposal to England requesting a land grant to create an Indian school that would be an academy and a college. Wheelock's Indian protégé, Samuel Occum, spent three years on a fundraising mission to England and Scotland, returning with over £12,000 for the Indian school. However, Wheelock eventually became disillusioned with his Indian students and decided to relocate to New Hampshire where he had obtained a land grant for a college. During the decade of the 1770s, Dartmouth educated about forty Indians and three times as many White students. By 1774, all the money Occum had collected for Indian education was spent (Wright, 1988).

Structure and Governance

Although it is often assumed that colonial colleges were modeled after the English universities of Oxford and Cambridge, that comparison is valid only in a limited sense. Thelin (2004) describes the English universities as "distinctive in their governance and formal legal structures" (p. 8). The English colleges within each university were privately endowed and tied to the university as part of a federation. Although the university was the formal, legal, degree-granting institution, the residential colleges within the universities were relatively autonomous and each was proud of its distinctive heritage, tradition, and emphasis. The colonial colleges, however, remained as single entities that "fused instruction with certification—a practice wholly alien to Oxford and Cambridge," and, although most were residential in nature, not all aspired to that model (pp. 8–9).

Colonial colleges also differed from their English counterparts in their governance structure. Rather than empower self-perpetuating associations of faculty, the colonial founders followed the Scottish model in which power was centered in an external board who vested administra-

tive authority in the president and to whom the president reported.

This pattern of governance was promulgated in the Harvard Charter of 1650, which provided for a president, treasurer, and five fellows. The authority of the corporation rested on the approval of the overseers, a board composed of government administrators and ministers. In effect, two groups were established to govern. The corporation was responsible for the administration of the college but was, in turn, responsible to the board of overseers. The substantial influence of the board in the community provided the support the college needed to survive and flourish (Cremin, 1970; Harvard Charter of 1650). This structure, rooted in Scottish universities and replicated by other colonial colleges, represented a sharp break from the English models of Oxford and Cambridge and defined the governance model prominent in contemporary America (Thelin, 2004, pp. 1, 11). The vast majority of college presidents during the colonial period were clergymen who also served in the classroom, often teaching the graduating class. The first non-clergyman president was John Leverett at Harvard in 1708, the second was John Wheelock at Dartmouth in 1779, and the third was Josiah Quincy at Harvard in 1829 (Rudolph, 1962, p. 170).

For most of the period between 1636 and 1800, the institutions were stable with the exception of the years during which the Revolutionary War was fought. Most faculties supported the cause of independence and many were active in military service or spoke out or wrote in favor of the cause. Some served in political office. Wartime activity took a toll on the colleges and the majority were dislocated or damaged by invading or defending armies. Harvard became army headquarters during the siege of Boston in 1775; American troops occupied King's College and used it as a hospital in 1776 (the trustees did not recover the building until 1783); the College of Rhode Island served as a barracks for American militia in 1776 and was later occupied and used as a hospital by the French; the British occupied Queens College in 1776; over a period of two years, the College of Philadelphia was occupied, first by the militia and then by the British. Yale escaped damage when the British invaded New Haven in 1779. Princeton was not as fortunate. In 1776, Princeton was seized by the British and used as a base of operations. The Americans

employed cannon fire to dislodge them and proceeded to occupy Nassau Hall themselves, eventually using the college as a military hospital. By the time officials regained use of the facilities, the college and church were ruined (Robson, 1985, pp. 111–119).

Tutors/Faculty and Curriculum

During the 17th century and the first half of the 18th, instructional staffs were composed primarily of tutors. They were young men, often in their late teens, who were preparing for careers in the ministry and had recently received their baccalaureate degrees. Responsible for both instruction and pastoral care, the hope was that one tutor would stay with one class through all four years. Most, however, moved on to careers before their charges graduated. Prior to 1685, only six of forty-one tutors remained at Harvard for more than three years. During the last half of the 18th century, faculty careers began to develop as a small group of permanent faculty, the professors, began to supplement the tutors and, at Harvard, tutors began to teach one subject to all classes. Prior to 1750, there were only 10 professors in all American colonial higher education, most of whom were at either Harvard or William and Mary. By 1795, that number was 105 and the number of colleges had slightly more than doubled. In all, about 200 individuals served as professors in nineteen colleges between 1750 and 1800 (Carrell, Morison, & Smith, cited in Finkelstein, 1983, p. 81).

Natural philosophy
study of nature and the
physical universe

Professorships began to develop at Harvard during the 1720s when two Hollis Professorships were endowed: one in divinity and the other in mathematics and **natural philosophy.** By 1750, the president was supported by three permanent professors and one permanent tutor. Four additional professorships were endowed before the end of the 18th century (Smith, cited in Finkelstein, 1983). The instructional staff was responsible for delivering a prescribed curriculum. There were no electives or separate professional programs. The belief was that, in the liberal arts, there was a fixed body of knowledge which constituted "absolute and immutable truth" passed down from antiquity and through the Middle Ages, the Renaissance, and the Reformation. That knowledge was to be absorbed, not questioned (Brubacher & Rudy, 1976, p. 13). The majority of colonial colleges through the early decades of the 18th century essentially followed the Harvard Programme of

1723, which, "except for the presence of a fourth year, the reviewing of classic authors in the first year, the addition of geography, the dropping of history and botany, and the increased attention paid to physics, [was] essentially the same program which President Dunster inaugurated in the early 17th century" (Potter, 1944, pp. 1–2). The general program of study is described in the vernacular below:

1. While ye students are Freshmen, they commonly recite ye Grammars, & [wth] them a Recitation in Tully, Virgil, ye Greek Testame[t] on Mondays, Tuesdays, [w]enesdays & Thursdays in ye morning & forenoon; on Friday mornings, Dugard's or Farnaby's Rhetoric[k], and on Saturday morning ye Greek Catachism, and towards ye latter end of ye year they dispute on Ramus's Definitions, [m]ondays and Tuesdays in ye Forenoon.

2. The Sophomores recite Burgersdicius's Logic[k], and a Manuscript called *New Logic[k]* in ye mornings & Forenoons; and towards ye latter end of ye year, Herebord's Meletemata, and dispute Mondays and Tuesdays in ye Forenoon; continuing also to recite ye Classic Authors with ye Logic[ks] & natural [Phylosophy]; on Saturday mornings they recite Wollebius's Divinity.

3. The Junr Sophisters recite Herebord's Meletemata, [mr] Morton's Physic[ks], More's Ethic[ks], Geography, Metaphysic[ks], in ye mornings & Forenoons; Wollebius on Saturday morning, dispute Mondays and Tuesdays in ye Forenoons.

4. The Senr Sophisters, besides Arithemetic[k], recite Allsted's Geometry, Gassendus's Astronomy in ye morning; go over ye Arts towards ye latter end of ye year, Ames's Medulla on Saturdays, dispute once a week. (Wadsworth, cited in Potter, 1944, p. 2)

Syllogistic logic
formal analysis of logical terms and structures in order to infer the truth from a set of premises

Disputation was an integral part of academic life and was intended to strengthen the mind and prepare the young man to think logically and speak with authority. The disputes were conducted in Latin and followed the rules of **syllogistic logic**. Following those detailed rules, the tutor would announce the question or proposition to be debated; one student (the respondent) would affirm or deny it, defend his position, and answer all arguments against that position made by the appointed opponents.

This same exercise was a highlight of commencement ceremonies, when roles were assigned by the president to members of the graduating class, generally in recognition of academic achievement. Topics included:

- Logic is the art of reasoning. Harvard, 1678, 1717, 1776
- Logic is the art of thinking and reasoning rightly. Yale, 1763
- Logic is the art of reasoning well for the purpose of finding truth and communicating it to others. Brown, 1769, 1776, 1786, 1796
- All simple ideas are clear. Yale, 1720
- The mind does not always think. Yale, 1783
- Matter cannot think. Brown, 1786
- Rhetoric is the art of illuminating the truth fully and elegantly. Princeton, 1750. (Potter, 1944, pp. 13, 16–19)

Syllogistic disputation
formalized method of debate incorporating the use of syllogisms

Forensic disputation
formalized method of debate that allows ethical, emotional, and logical arguments

Use of the **syllogistic disputation** declined during the latter part of the 18th century as students were required to practice it with less frequency. At the same time, use of the **forensic disputation** increased. Forensic disputes might be the type made in public assemblies or courts where several people speak in support of, or against, any person or thing. This style of argumentation lacked traditional academic form and standardization. It differed from the syllogistic exercise "in its denial of the restrictive yoke of the syllogism, its inclusion of ethical and pathetic proof as well as logical, its freedom from the scholastic subtleties of language, and its use of English in place of traditional Latin" (Potter, 1944, p. 38). Several topics debated at Princeton commencements from 1760 to 1774 illustrate common themes:

- The Elegance of an Oration much consists in the Words being consonant to the Sense. 1760
- No Man can be a comple[ate] Orator without a universal Acquaintance with the Arts and Sciences. 1761
- Ridicule…[is] not a test of the truth. 1769
- A mixed Monarchy is the best Form of Government. 1772
- Every human Art is not only consistent with true Religion, but receives its highest Improvement from it. 1773. (Williams, cited in Potter, 1944, pp. 44–46)

Contemporary issues were considered during the period of the Revolution. Examples of problems consid-

ered by Yale undergraduates from January 1 to December 16, 1782, included:

- Whether the Press ought to be free?
- Whether female Academies would be beneficial?
- Whether there is a Vacuum beyond the Atmosphere?
- Whether the manner of English Settlement of America and become possessed of Indian territory be justifiable by the Law of Nature & Nations?
- Whether the Long Isld Trade with the British be justifiable during the present war? (Stiles, cited in Potter, 1944, pp. 46–47)

Students were expected to read scripture and attend worship services on Sunday. In the mid-1700s, the Yale curriculum continued to be much like the Harvard curriculum of the mid-1600s:

> The first year established language skills—tools; the second year provided depth in the study of logic—a method, another tool; during the third and fourth years, these skills and method were turned on the advanced subjects— natural philosophy [physics], mathematics, and metaphysics—one at a time. And during all four years, every Friday and Saturday, all Yale students recited and disputed the key subjects—divinity and ethics. On Sunday the college worshipped together, and what may have appeared to be a day off for the curriculum was really the day when the curriculum fell into place, with the assistance of prayer, sermon, and Biblical explication from the president of Yale. (Rudolph, 1977, pp. 32–33)

Throughout the second half of the 18th century, significant change began to occur. The sciences of botany, chemistry, anatomy, and physiology appeared at those colleges that offered a medical course as well as the bachelor's. In 1796, Princeton appointed the first professor of chemistry in a liberal arts program without a medical course. As interest in science grew, the colleges sought to contain and direct it through the transformation of the final year of divinity study into a course in moral philosophy (ethics). Usually taught by the president, the course brought together ethics, science, and religion to determine how men should behave in an effort to understand morality as a function of reason and human nature (Rudolph, 1977, pp. 39–42). Major changes occurred at William and Mary under the direction of Thomas Jefferson. As a member of the board of visitors, Jefferson reorganized the college

Natural history
study of plants and animals

Enlightenment
intellectual movement in Europe that promoted reason as a way to understand the universe and the human condition

Academies
postsecondary institutions that often taught liberal arts and practical skills to some degree

by abolishing the professorships of divinity and oriental languages and adding professorships in public adminis-tration, modern languages, and medical science. Shifting the curriculum from a religious to a secular purpose, he included study in **natural history**, natural philosophy, natural and international law, and fine arts. Other colonial colleges experimented with new curriculum as well and shifted back and forth to some degree with the changing times. Presiding as provost at the College of Philadelphia, William Smith designed a curriculum that included elec-tives in German, Spanish, Italian, fencing, military science, and dancing. The European **Enlightenment** emphasized the natural sciences and broke down natural philosophy into mathematics, chemistry, natural history, and geogra-phy. New texts, written in English, eliminated the reliance on Latin as the language of instruction. As the curriculum moved from explaining the ways to God to understanding man, interest in orations, history, poetry, literature, reason, and observation grew (Rudolph, 1977, pp. 48–53).

Thomas Woody's (1929) seminal work on the educa-tion of women describes educational opportunities for girls during the colonial period as limited in terms of accessi-bility and substance. When it was available at all, a girl's education was generally confined to reading, writing, and arithmetic. This minimal approach reflected the gener-ally accepted view that female minds were inferior and a woman's appropriate focus was the home. Consequently, valuable skills were domestic in nature (such as sewing, knitting, cleaning), and many believed that educating a woman was a wasted effort, for an educated woman would make a poor wife (pp. 1:92–93). Although these attitudes were occasionally questioned by advocates of women's edu-cation, it was not until the Ursuline Convent for girls was established in New Orleans in 1727 that effective efforts to improve girls' education began to develop. Other **acade-mies** and seminaries followed, and between 1750 and 1865, they became the prevailing type of educational institution for girls (p. 1:108). The aims of the early female academies were to prepare students for life, unlike the Latin gram-mar schools whose primary objective had been to prepare young men for college. Throughout the period between 1750 and 1870, various elements of "life preparation" were offered, including "Christian religion and morals, domestic training, maternal influence and social usefulness, train-

ing for the teaching profession, accomplishments, physical health, intellectual enjoyment, and mental discipline" (p. 1:397). The central two objectives, however, were religious and domestic training.

Students and Student Life

Admission to Harvard College could be considered when "any Scholar is able to Read Tully or such like classic Latin Author *ex tempore*, and make and speak true Latin in verse and *prose suo (ut aiunt) Marte*, and decline perfectly the paradigms of Nouns and verbs in the Greek tongue, then may he be admitted to the College" (Statutes of Harvard, 1646, p. 125). Consequently, formal training with a minister or master was often necessary prior to attendance.

Since a college degree was not required for the majority of occupations in early America, student populations were very small. The students themselves were young, often between 16 and 17 years old in their first year. Estimates indicate that probably no more than one in every thousand colonists enrolled in any college in existence before 1776 and fewer actually graduated. Fewer than 600 students attended Harvard during the whole of the 17th century, and only about 465 graduated. Its largest pre-Revolutionary graduating class in 1771 celebrated 63 metriculants. Yale enrolled only 36 students in 1710 and 338 in 1770. Between 1677 and 1703, the majority of students at Harvard were sons of clergymen followed by sons of merchants, shopkeepers, master mariners, magistrates, attorneys, militia officers, and wealthy farmers; but sons of ordinary men such as artisans, seamen, servants, and poor farmers attended as well. As rising costs in the 18th century required students who could pay tuition, attendance began to be restricted to sons of the wealthy. Most schools, however, continued charity scholarships and some allowed poor students to teach school on a part-time basis in order to earn money for tuition (Lucas, 2006, pp. 108–109).

Student life was rather dull. College libraries contained few, if any, contemporary novels or periodicals, the company of women was forbidden, and athletic programs did not exist. Students looked to each other for entertainment and created college literary and debating societies, many of which, in their early years, were religious in nature. The origin of American fraternities, which fully developed later and tended to be more social, can be traced to the

College of William and Mary, where several student groups formed, including one known primarily by its initials: F.H.C. (Flat Hat Club). It was not long before a rival group organized, in 1776, which was the first to become known by the initials of its Greek motto, ΦΒΚ (**Phi Beta Kappa**). The F.H.C. did not survive the Revolution. Although Phi Beta Kappa did not survive the British invasion of Virginia, the society was transplanted north to Yale and Harvard by one of its members and chapters were formed there. For some of these clubs, literary or oratory improvements were the goal, for others the object was entertainment. The Porcellian (or Pig Club) met to drink or dine and the Hasty Pudding Club, founded in 1795, was a "jolly amalgam of literary, convivial, and patriotic elements" and became the largest of the Harvard societies in the early 1800s (Morrison, 1936, pp. 181–183). There were two literary associations at the College of New Jersey in fall 1766. The object of one, the Well-Meaning Club, was "to collect the first young men in point of character and scholarship as its members." The object of the other, the Plain-Dealing Society, was to "outnumber the Well-Meaning," but the level of dissension between the two compelled the faculty to abolish both in 1769 (Williams, cited in Potter, 1944, p. 68). With the exception of the University of Pennsylvania, students formed debating and literary societies at all the colonial colleges prior to 1800. These groups supported the social activities of the students, in many cases helped them improve their debating skills, and allowed a structure through which students could create interesting libraries with contemporary publications.

Following the example of European colleges, colonial colleges were primarily residential, although students and faculty were rarely on friendly terms. Faculty were placed in the role of disciplinarian and expected to seek out and reprimand or punish students who broke the many rules that regulated nearly every facet of a student's life. The close regulation sometimes resulted in student rebellion, the earliest record of which occurred at Harvard in 1766. Known as the **Bad Butter Rebellion**, the conflict began over rancid butter in the commons but escalated into a major confrontation between students and overseers regarding numerous other complaints (Lucas, 2006, p. 112). Guilty students faced elaborate punishments including fines, suspension of privileges, suspension, or expulsion.

Phi Beta Kappa
founded in 1776, it is the nation's oldest honor society

Bad Butter Rebellion
one of the first student protests on record

John Adams
second president of the
United States

Hard liquor was banned, but students were allowed beer, wine, and ale, which no doubt contributed to misbehavior. The diary of **John Adams** recalls an evening in 1786 when "the syllogists [following a time-honored tradition] all got together...and drank until not one of them could stand straight, or was sensible of what he did. A little after 9 they sallied out, and for a quarter of an hour made such a noise as might be heard at a mile distant.... Mr. _____ had two squares of his window broke" (Adams's Diary, cited in Potter, 1944, p. 14). No doubt the college disciplinarians were busy the following day.

GLOSSARY

New England: Northeast area of the United States; includes Maine, Vermont, Massachusetts, New Hampshire, Connecticut, and Rhode Island

Puritans: Christian religious group that left England seeking religious freedom

Colonial colleges: nine colleges founded during the colonial period

Disputation: formalized method of debate

Toleration: willingness to allow various Protestant religious denominations

Great Awakening: religious movement around the 1730s

Natural philosophy: study of nature and the physical universe

Syllogistic logic: formal analysis of logical terms and structures in order to infer the truth from a set of premises

Syllogistic disputation: formalized method of debate incorporating the use of syllogisms

Forensic disputation: formalized method of debate that allows ethical, emotional, and logical arguments

Natural history: study of plants and animals

Enlightenment: intellectual movement in Europe that promoted reason as a way to understand the universe and the human condition

Academies: postsecondary institutions that often taught liberal arts and practical skills to some degree

Phi Beta Kappa: founded in 1776, it is the nation's oldest honor society

Bad Butter Rebellion: one of the first student protests on record

John Adams: second president of the United States

CHAPTER THREE

Growth and Change, 1800–1900

The New Century

In 1800, the United States of America was between wars. Having recently won independence, the young nation would soon face Britain again in the War of 1812. America was growing and expanding. There were numerous and varied opportunities for economic development and individuals could improve their economic position with or without a college degree. Industrialization, westward expansion, and the belief that the common man could be successful through persistence and hard work created a society that looked to the future with high expectations. Frederick Rudolph (1962) expressed the effect of this national attitude on higher education:

> A country that was hurrying into the future needed colleges that would hurry along with it. The American colleges would therefore experience the same challenges as political parties, state constitutions and economic institutions. They would be asked to pass a test of utility. They would have to answer the question of whether they were serving the needs of a people whose interest in yesterday hardly existed, and whose interest in today was remark-

ably limited to its usefulness for getting to tomorrow. (pp. 110-111)

Rapid expansion of higher education during the 1800s can only be understood within the context of the exponential growth and dramatic social changes experienced by the country. During the 19th century the population grew from about 5.3 million to 72.2 million (U.S. Census Bureau, 2010, "1800"; U.S. Census, 2010, "1900"). The influx of immigrants was so great that by the early 1900s, about 1 in 6 Americans was foreign born (Miller & Miller, 1996, p. 68). The growing population spread out into the twenty-nine new states added to the Union between 1800 and 1900 as the western border moved to the Pacific coast. The territory far west of the Mississippi offered gold and silver. The old European inheritance practice that promised the eldest son the family property no longer bound young men to their parents. Land was cheap and almost everywhere in abundance. Victory over the British in the War of 1812 established the United States of America as an international force, renewed national pride, and encouraged a personal commitment to the good of the Republic. Over the course of the century, railroads would replace dusty trails, canals would connect the waterways, and steamboats would navigate the Mississippi River connecting the Gulf of Mexico deep into the interior of the country. Access to and through the Great Lakes connected the heartland to the Atlantic. Industrialization created a manufacturing base, providing economic security for many. Progress was marked by financial success, innovation, and invention. On the one hand, the notion that in a democracy each man could accomplish anything with ambition and hard work was true for many, and particularly true for men who were White and Protestant. On the other hand, native people were dislocated and driven from their ancestral lands; women, immigrants, and children worked long, stressful hours in factories; many people, including miners and railroad workers, labored in unsafe environments for little pay; and prejudice against immigrant newcomers was common, making it very difficult for some to work at all. For most of the century, slavery was legal, causing incredible suffering to those forced to endure it. Over 600,000 soldiers lost their lives in the **Civil War** as it decimated significant parts of the country (McPherson, 1982, p. 488). Although the war succeeded in maintaining the Union and free-

Civil War

war between the American states from 1861 to 1865

ing those enslaved, voting rights continued to be limited. Opportunity did not bless all equally.

For some, education offered the prospect of new possibilities. During the 19th century, the elementary and secondary school system developed and higher education began to expand. Religious diversity and a changing orientation toward religion had an impact on college and curriculum development, sometimes moving in a conservative direction and sometimes pushing the boundaries toward a more secular and scientific purpose. One hundred eighty-two "permanent" colleges were legally founded, and it is estimated that hundreds of others opened and failed prior to the beginning of the Civil War in 1861 (Tewksbury, 1932). Locally based, these small **liberal arts** colleges offered accessibility to students who did not have the means to travel far from home. The proliferation of private educational academies alongside colleges is worthy of note, as they were similar institutions that offered post-secondary education designed to prepare a person for life. Theoretically expected to offer practical subjects, more often than not academies followed the form of the classical curriculum. Study of the classics continued to be considered by many students and parents as the most advantageous course in terms of personal and professional success. Academies and small colleges tended to rise up along the frontier as the population settled. Supported by local communities, these institutions provided a sense of settled privilege and prestige. Although they were not large, they could also have a positive impact on the economic base of the region if they were well attended, particularly if students boarded and ate in town (Church & Sedlak, 1976, pp. 23–50). It has been estimated that around 1850, the U.S. population was about 23 million. There were over 6,000 academies enrolling more than 250,000 students; about that same time, there were 239 colleges enrolling about 25,000 students. Approximately 4 million children (roughly 56% of the age-appropriate population) were enrolled in public common schools. The educational system was gearing up but, even so, estimates indicate that at mid-century only about 1.25% of the college age population (20- to 24-year-olds) was enrolled (Barnard, Fishlow, cited in Church & Sedlak, 1976, pp. 36–38).

Although compulsory school laws did exist during the colonial period, they were rarely enforced. For most

Liberal arts

originally included grammar, dialectic, rhetoric, arithmetic, geometry, music, and astronomy

**Compulsory
Education Law**

law requiring school
attendance, first passed in
1852 in Massachusetts

Preparatory departments

remedial instruction, offered
in college, to prepare
students for college-level
studies

Legal precedent

legal principle, decided by a
court, which provides
authority that other courts
may follow

of the population, the purpose of education was to teach the young to read so they could know the Bible. That accomplished, there was little demand or need for more. However, the growth of higher education during the 1800s was encouraged by the movement to develop a lower-level public school system. The first American **Compulsory Education Law** was passed in Massachusetts in 1852. Other states followed. During this period, prior to the Civil War, colleges were adapting to the needs of the country by expanding science and mathematics offerings, including **preparatory departments**, offering parallel courses, and providing instruction in areas outside the traditional classical curriculum. These efforts made the institutions and higher education more accessible to middle-class students of fairly modest means (Potts, 1977).

Public/Private Distinction:
The Dartmouth College Case

Even though there are varying opinions about its importance and effect at the time, the decision in the Dartmouth College case is often credited with first describing the distinction between private and public institutions and, consequently, making possible the tremendous growth of private institutions in the 1800s. The case also set an important **legal precedent** in the area of constitutional law in the United States. The summary of events and short brief of the case presented below is based on the work of John King Lord (1913) and the U.S. Supreme Court case *Trustees of Dartmouth College v. Woodward, 17 U.S. (4 Wheat.) 518 (1819).*

> *May 1815:* John Wheelock (president of Dartmouth College) and the twelve-member board of trustees to which he reported held divergent opinions regarding a variety of issues. Their disagreements became public when two anonymous pamphlets were widely circulated that were extremely critical of the trustees and asserted that they were trying to increase the strength and influence of their religious denomination at the college to the detriment of the political independence of the people. It was generally believed that President Wheelock was the author. The publication of the pamphlets was followed in June by another published statement (clearly authored by Wheelock) that repeated his general complaints against the trustees and requested the intervention of the legislature. A special committee of ten members of the state

legislature met to consider the matter. Wheelock wanted the college board of trustees to be increased by at least six members, who could be selected to strengthen his influence and control. The committee recommended an investigation and three individuals were selected to go to Dartmouth and examine the charges. The legislature adjourned for the year.

August 16, 1815: The investigating committee and the college trustees met at Hanover in Wheelock's house for two and a half days. The charges of both sides were reviewed and the committee tried unsuccessfully to negotiate a resolution. The meeting was adjourned.

August 25, 1815: The trustees themselves had also conducted an investigation and reported that as far as they were concerned, the pamphlets had been written by Wheelock. The president was notified of their report by mail. Wheelock responded in writing that he did recognize their jurisdiction in the matter but would be pleased to be judged by the legislature whom he recognized as having ultimate authority over the institution by virtue of the institutional charter originally granted by King George III, the authority for which, Wheelock believed, had transferred to the state of New Hampshire after the Revolution.

August 26, 1815: The college trustees voted to remove John Wheelock from his office as president of the college, from his position on the board, and from his position as a faculty member. A variety of complaints were lodged against him including charges that he played a part in the writing, circulation, and publication of the two anonymous pamphlets that the trustees felt spread lies about the institution and were libelous; that he was not effective in disciplinary issues; that he was guilty of fraud in the administration of certain funds; and that he was spreading rumors that religious differences were at the heart of the trustees' problems with him (they strongly denied this). Two of the college's trustees (including one who was the governor of New Hampshire) voted against Wheelock's removal based on the belief that the charges against him were not proven.

August 28, 1815: The college trustees elected the Reverend Francis Brown to the position of president. Wheelock wrote to express his opinion that the action of the board was illegal and inoperative. Regardless, Brown accepted the position and was installed on September 27th. No one seriously contended that the trustees did not have the authority to remove Wheelock and even the board's opponents in the legislature recognized Reverend Brown as the legal president.

March 1816: The Democrats won both branches of the legislature and the governor's office from the Federalists. Wheelock was a Democrat with numerous Federalist supporters.

June 1816: The new governor clearly stated his lack of support for the college trustees. A second committee was formed by the legislature to make recommendations concerning the college problem and to reconsider the report prepared by the first group of visiting investigators. The first report, favorable to the college trustees, was still at the printer when the second committee produced a bill which recommended that, since it would be difficult to determine all the facts and resolve the pending issues, it would be advisable to simply change the charter in order to solve the problem. The "Act to amend, enlarge and improve the Corporation of Dartmouth College" provided that the name be changed to Dartmouth University; that the number of trustees should be twenty-one, the majority of which would be required for a quorum; and that a board of overseers composed of twenty-five individuals should be established. The board of overseers would have authority over the board of trustees and, ultimately, the college. The president of the New Hampshire senate and the speaker of the house of representatives of New Hampshire were to be included on the board of overseers. The governor and council were authorized to fill all vacancies on the board of overseers and, until its first meeting, on the board of trustees as well.

In effect, this decision transferred substantial governing authority to the state. Regardless of efforts by the college trustees to intervene, the act passed on essentially a party line vote: Federalists 84 against; Democrats 96 in favor and 2 against. Efforts to postpone the bill to determine if it conflicted with the **contract clause** of the U.S. Constitution failed. After much discussion, the college trustees decided they would not abide by the act until after all their claims against it had been decided in the courts. They regretted they had not also dismissed Judge William Woodward. Named as the defendant in the lawsuit, he had been the secretary and treasurer of the college board of trustees and, as a supporter of Wheelock, had in his possession the college seal and all the records.

August 1816: The governor and the new *university* trustees came to town to hold their first board meeting and take authority over the college, but no one had made arrangements for the meeting and no rooms were reserved. A number of extraordinarily polite letters were hand carried back and forth between the governor and President Brown that morning as the new trustees tried to secure a campus location to hold their meeting. The governor

---

Contract clause

Article 1, section 10, clause 1 of the U.S. Constitution prohibits states from enacting any law impairing the obligation of contracts

decided they might try to meet in the library but they could not gain access. One of the college professors, who also served as librarian, claimed that President Brown had the key to the library meeting room. Brown finally responded that he had no objection to the group holding the meeting in the library but he, as president, had no authority over the library rooms and could not, therefore, provide access. The meeting was finally held in Judge Woodward's office, although one new member was too sick to attend and only one member of the old board was present. As a result, the group was one short of a quorum. They again wrote to President Brown, this time requesting his attendance as a board member. His written refusal very politely stated that the trustees as composed by the original charter had not yet reached a decision regarding their acceptance of the act and thus he could not attend. The next day was commencement day. Early in the morning, the governor summoned two college professors to inquire and instruct the new trustees on their roles at commencement. The two professors very politely replied that they did not think they should meet with the "assembled gentlemen" as the group did not have the quorum necessary to act as trustees.

At the same time, President Brown and the *college* trustees were meeting at President Brown's house and decided that they would not recognize the new charter. They communicated their intentions to the governor. The *university* board responded with a long written protest but there was little they could do.

The new *university* trustees laid out an elaborate plan for the university organization and adjourned.

December 1816: The governor and other interested parties took a new approach. They managed to have legislation passed that reduced the number of attendees necessary for a quorum and authorized the governor to convene both the *university* board of trustees and the board of overseers. In addition, the bill called for financial penalties against anyone who continued to operate outside the parameters of the act that had amended the charter. Despite the challenges this presented, most on the *college* board held fast.

February 4, 1817: The *university* board met and reached its new quorum requirement by February 6th. They summoned President Brown and the two professors who had been appointed to the *university* board. All refused to appear, although they responded in writing.

February 22, 1817: The *university* trustees removed Brown and the two uncooperative professors from the *university* board. Within several months, the other members of the old college board were also removed. In February, John

Wheelock was named president of *Dartmouth University* and new faculty were appointed.

The *university* trustees tried to get the keys to the chapel and the library as the new term was scheduled to begin shortly. Their request refused, they broke into the chapel and changed the lock; they did the same at Dartmouth Hall and the library.

March 3, 1817: The spring term was scheduled to begin on March 3rd. By this time, the *college* trustees had filed a legal suit against William Woodward for the return of the seal and the records. The term for students of Dartmouth College began the next day in rented rooms above a hat store near the college property. Most all of the 130 students reported there. The term for Dartmouth University opened on March 5th with 7 in attendance, only 1 of whom was a student.

April 4, 1817: At the age of 63, John Wheelock died. He left an estate estimated at $20,000 to the *university,* with the condition that the donation would be cancelled if the act creating the university was voided.

June 12, 1817: The *university* trustees appointed the Reverend William Allen, Wheelock's son-in-law, to the presidency. At this point, the two presidents were President Brown of Dartmouth College and President Allen of Dartmouth University.

August 27, 1817: This was the date both the *college* and the *university* planned for commencement. Many people were concerned and anticipated "great difficulties" and "collisions." The students, the majority of whom had remained sympathetic to the cause of the *college*, staged what might be one of the first sit-ins as they took control of the meetinghouse. More than sixty young men armed with clubs, canes, and stones held the meeting house for three days and three nights. In the end, the *college* held its commencement ceremony in the meeting house; the *university* held its ceremony in the chapel. The *college* graduated 39 bachelor's and 11 medical students; the *university* graduated 8 bachelor's and 9 medical students. Most of the crowd turned up for the *college,* as it was still far better attended.

November 6, 1817: The New Hampshire Superior Court found unanimously against the *college*. The *college* continued and pressed on to the U.S. Supreme Court. However, when the news of the state court's decision reached Dartmouth the most serious conflict of the whole affair took place. Again it involved students. The *university* faculty decided it was time to take over the libraries of the two great student literary societies: the Social Friends and the United Fraternity. The societies' libraries were on the second floor of Dartmouth Hall. The institutional library (which was separate from the libraries of the literary societies) amounted to about 4,000 books, many of which were obsolete texts and duplicates. Together, the literary societies' libraries held approximately the same number and were far more valuable to the students. Fearing that the *university* would confiscate their books, the students had moved many of them and packed others. However, on November 11th, several *university* faculty members and allied students arrived with an ax and broke through the door of one of the student libraries while the others stood guard with clubs raised. Students heard the commotion and assembled in great numbers, rang the alarm, and armed themselves with clubs from a pile of wood. The intruders, now inside the library, defended themselves with the ax through the hole in the door. The *university* group was greatly outnumbered but, fortunately, the incident ended without injury and the intruders were escorted from the building. The literary societies expelled the offending individuals from their ranks.

March 1818: The case was heard in the U.S. Supreme Court. Lead counsel for the *college* trustees was Dartmouth alumnus Daniel Webster (class of 1801).

February 1, 1819: The U.S. Supreme Court found in favor of the trustees of Dartmouth College. According to the court, the New Hampshire act violated the U.S. Constitution's contract clause, and the original charter was legally binding. The institution belonged to the *college* trustees according to the governance structure outlined in the charter, not to the *university* trustees through the structure as decreed by the legislature. The *university* trustees were forced to withdraw from the college buildings (although they refused to turn over the keys) and the institution then known as Dartmouth University ceased to exist.

Trustees of Dartmouth College v. Woodward, 17 U.S. (4 Wheat.) 518 (1819)

This was the first case involving higher education to reach the U.S. Supreme Court. The action was brought by the trustees of the college against William Woodward (representing the state of New Hampshire) in the state court of New Hampshire for the "records, corporate seal, and other corporate property, to which the plaintiffs (the *college* trustees) allege themselves to be entitled." Prior to reaching the U.S. Supreme Court, the case had been decided by the New

Hampshire Superior Court, which found in favor of the defendant (Woodward) in support of the state. After examining the case, the U.S. Supreme Court noted: "The single question now to be considered is do the acts to which the verdict [of the New Hampshire Superior Court] refers violate the Constitution of the United States? If the acts passed by the legislature of New Hampshire on June 27 and December 18, 1816, are valid, then the court would find for the state (defendant). Relevant facts of the case:

1. The title of the plaintiffs (the Dartmouth *College* trustees) originated in a charter dated December 13, 1769, in which twelve persons were named to serve as the trustees of Dartmouth College. They were granted the usual corporate privileges and powers and authorized to govern the college. They were also authorized to fill vacancies created in their own body.

2. The New Hampshire legislature had passed three acts amending the charter. Among the changes (not all inclusive) were:

June 27, 1816

Changed the name to Dartmouth University.

Increased the number of trustees to twenty-one, the majority of whom would represent a quorum, and gave the appointment of the additional trustees to the executive of the state (governor).

Created a board of overseers, composed of twenty-five persons, fifteen of whom would represent a quorum. This board would have extensive authority including the power to inspect and control the actions of the trustees. The board of overseers would include the president of the New Hampshire State Senate and the Speaker of the House of Representatives of New Hampshire. The board was to be appointed by the governor and the council of New Hampshire, who were also empowered to fill all vacancies.

December 18, 1816

The governor was authorized to summon meetings of the university trustees and the board of overseers.

The number necessary for a quorum was reduced to nine for the board of trustees and six votes

were set as the required number necessary for the passage of any act or resolution.

December 26, 1816

Established a $500 fine, per offense, for acting against the "act to amend and enlarge and improve the corporation of Dartmouth College."

In order to decide whether or not the action of the legislature violated the U.S. Constitution, the U.S. Supreme Court had to determine:

1. Is the charter a contract? If so, is the contract protected by the U.S. Constitution?
2. Does the action of the legislature impair the contract as the plaintiffs (college trustees) contend?

In order to determine whether or not this contract was protected by the U.S. Constitution, the U.S. Supreme Court considered two issues: the nature of the term *contract* and the nature of *incorporation*. The decision of the court:

1. The charter is a contract, the obligations of which cannot be impaired without violating the Constitution of the United States.
2. The crown (England) granted the charter as it was written and the duties to honor it were passed to the people of New Hampshire after the Revolution. Consequently, the state cannot alter the contract.

It was understood that contracts involving property or some object of value to an individual were protected by the U.S. Constitution. The U.S. Supreme Court held that the trustees, representing the donors who funded the institution for a particular purpose based on the structure outlined in the charter, had a vested interest in the assets of the corporation. The corporation represented the will of the donors as stated in the charter, just as if each individual was represented. The court concluded that this was a private corporation, but also recognized that the situation might be different in other circumstances. If, for instance, the act of incorporation was a grant of political power, if it created a civil institution to be employed in the administration of the government, if the funds of the college were public property, or if the state of New Hampshire, as a government, was the only party interested in these transactions, then it may be that the legislature of the state could act according to its own judgment, unrestrained by any

limitation of its power by the Constitution of the United States. The court considered the purpose of the Dartmouth corporation, noting that "education is the object of national concern, and a proper subject of legislation." Although the U.S. Supreme Court recognized Dartmouth as a private corporation, it also noted that the government had a legitimate role in education and left open the possibility "that there may be an institution founded by government, and placed entirely under its immediate control, the officers of which would be public officers, amenable exclusively to government."

Scholars disagree on the importance of the case to the public/private distinction in higher education. Some note that even after the decision, state governments continued to support denominational colleges (including Dartmouth) and that the public/private distinction did not really take shape until after the Civil War. Contemporary scholar Jurgen Herbst argues that the decision was the culmination of legal issues from the colonial period through 1819, and that the decision laid the legal foundation on which our current system of higher education rests (Whitehead & Herbst, 1986). Whether the impact was immediate or delayed, whether it intentionally established a public/private distinction in education or not, the justices did succeed in interpreting the contract clause so as to define and protect private institutions and business corporations from government interference.

The Yale Report of 1828

The Yale Report of 1828 was prepared by the faculty at Yale College as an examination of the classical curriculum. Scholars disagree about whether it was a conservative document lauding the benefits of the classical course in order to resist change or whether it was a treatise in support of educational progress. Openly debating the purpose of education, the report considered whether education should be primarily concerned with passing knowledge from one generation to the next, or whether it should serve a more utilitarian purpose. The faculty explain: "In laying down the foundation of a thorough education, it is necessary that all the important mental faculties be brought into exercise…. In the course of instruction in this college, it has been an object to maintain such a proportion between the different branches of literature and science, as to form in

the student a proper balance of character" (p. 192). They argue that "eloquence and solid learning should go together," for "to what purpose has a man become deeply learned, if he has no faculty of communicating his knowledge? And of what use is a display of rhetorical elegance, from one who knows little or nothing which is worth communicating?" (pp. 192–193). While allowing that professional and technical education had its place, the faculty held that the "prescribed course contains those subjects only which ought to be understood, as we think, by everyone who aims at a thorough education. They are not the peculiarities of any profession or art. These are to be learned in the professional and practical schools. But the principles of science are the common foundations of all high intellectual attainments.... so in a college, all should be instructed in those branches of knowledge, of which no one destined to the higher walks of life ought to be ignorant" (p. 195). Education should exercise a form of mental discipline that would train the faculties for their use, as "the two great points to be gained in intellectual culture are the *discipline* and the *furniture* of the mind; expanding its powers and storing it with knowledge" (p. 192).

The report had a significant impact on colleges at the time, as it "reconciled the financial interests of the schools and the cultural pretensions of the teachers with the practical tendencies of a developing nation and reconciled, perhaps more importantly, the conflict within parents and students between the desire to share the cultural training of the elite and the desire for practical training for the business of life" (Church & Sedlak, 1976, p. 33).

Institutional Diversification

During the 19th century, higher education changed significantly. Many established institutions expanded both in size and scope to meet the demands of a rapidly developing nation. While some retained the old-time college atmosphere and continued to focus on the liberal arts with a strong religious foundation, others incorporated science into the curriculum and adopted a research orientation that emphasized the importance of using institutional resources to solve problems and advance society. Educational opportunities were offered to new populations of students. Hundreds of new institutions opened, while others closed. As higher education diversified, different types of institutions existed

side by side, each vying for students, financial support, and public opinion.

Traditional liberal arts colleges continued to spring up, along with towns, as communities sought to transplant culture onto the frontier. Rudolph (1962) equates the spirit of college founding in the 19th century to the same spirit that encouraged canal building, farming, and gold mining—a faith in the future and the "romantic belief in endless progress" (pp. 48–49). When America entered the Revolutionary War, there were 9 colleges; at the time of the Civil War there were about 250. A few decades later, the state of Ohio would have 37 institutions for a population of 3 million. The difficulties of travel tended to encourage the development of regional colleges, as did the missionary movement and the desire of settlers on the frontier to re-create their New England home towns. Most institutions were founded by various Protestant denominations, often with the blessing and gratitude of the community. The desire for a learned clergy to minister to the people and for the faithful to be educated according to the tenets of a particular denomination led to college founding by the Congregationalists of New England, in addition to the Methodists, Baptists, Lutherans, German Reformed, Dutch Reformed, and Unitarians. The Presbyterians, however, outdistanced all others. Just prior to the Civil War, they were operating or controlling over 25% of the colleges that would continue into the 20th century (Rudolph, 1962, pp. 44–58).

Women's Colleges

In the early part of the 19th century, women's lives were dictated and limited by their gender. If a woman chose to marry, she was no longer recognized under the law and thus became completely dependent on her husband. As a wife and mother, her responsibilities focused on the home and the creation and raising of children with strong Christian morals. The Revolution had expanded the role of motherhood, raising it to a national purpose of preparing the next generation of citizens and leaders for the new Republic. "Republican motherhood" required both virtue and education (Kerber, 1980). However, even with this expanded role, women could not vote or speak in public. They were expected to be a social conscience in a limited sense through participation in appropriate, often religion-based, organizations. In 1848, a group of forward-thinking women published the *Declaration of Sentiments* at the First Women's Rights Convention, which was held in Seneca Falls, New York. Women wanted recognition of married women under the law, a single standard of morality for men and women, fair wages for employed women, consideration of mothers as guardians of children in cases of divorce and separation, admission to men's colleges and professional schools, and the right to vote (U.S. Department of the Interior, n.d.).

Another national conflict, the Civil War, once again changed roles and opportunities for women. During the war, women served as nurses and doctors and filled certain positions that had traditionally been reserved for men. The census of 1870 included at least one woman in each of the 338 occupations listed; roughly one woman in eight of those over 10 years old was employed. However, 93% of all women workers were relegated to 1 of 7 occupations: domestic service, agricultural laborers, seamstresses, milliners, teachers, textile mill workers, and laundresses (Newcomer, 1959, p. 17). The devastation of the war resulted in fewer men of marrying age, forcing more women to find ways to sustain themselves. Westward expansion also presented opportunities for women, and the pioneer role did not easily support the traditional exclusionary protection afforded to women in more settled environments. As the immigrant population exploded and compulsory school attendance laws multiplied, the need for schools and teachers expanded as well.

Women were considered natural teachers, especially for the elementary level, and the occupation of teacher became an acceptable role for a single woman. From an economic perspective, this was a very practical approach since the salaries for male teachers were commonly two to four times those paid to female teachers. As the argument went, in order to function, a democratic nation needed an educated electorate. It was becoming more obvious that numerous female teachers were required in order to "get even a minimum universal education for male voters," and "since teachers must know at least as much as their pupils… it was necessary to concede that a very substantial number of the female population must be educated too" (Newcomer, 1959, p. 15). The social significance of educating women was expressed by many who believed that "the cheapest,

easiest, and surest road to universal education is to educate those who are to be mothers and teachers of future generations;…the proper training of women is the strategic point in the education of the race;…and educate a man and you have educated one person, educate a mother and you have educated a whole family" (McIver, cited in Woody, 1929, p. 1:403). The education of women could therefore serve two purposes: those who married and became mothers would be better prepared to assist in the formation of their own children; those women who did not marry could be teachers in the schools.

As a consequence of the growth of public elementary schools, many female seminaries and academies made teacher education one of their primary objectives. However, by the end of the 1830s, it became more obvious that these institutions would not be able to produce a sufficient number of teachers to meet the need. As early as 1826, a report of a committee of the New York State Senate noted the value of establishing separate schools specifically for teacher education. In Massachusetts, the Board of Education recognized a similar need and successfully opened the first **normal schools** there in 1829 (Woody, 1929, pp. 1:471–473). The normal school movement continued to grow as it spread across the country.

Normal school
designed to prepare teachers for the public school system

Throughout the second half of the 19th century, liberal arts colleges for women were established. The first of these institutions, Mount Holyoke, was founded in 1837 by Mary Lyon and began as a seminary in South Hadley, Massachusetts. Although the female seminary did not offer Greek, Latin, or the classical curriculum of the male academy, a select few maintained high standards and required original thought. Those institutions became the model for many other female seminaries and eventually some coeducational colleges. Mount Holyoke determined "to turn daughters who were acted upon into women capable of self-propelled action" (Horowitz, 1984, p. 12). As a result, Mount Holyoke and another noteworthy women's academy, Ipswich in Massachusetts, provided female leaders for the future colleges of Vassar and Wellesley. The opening of Vassar College in 1861 provided a significant new opportunity in that it offered the full college liberal arts curriculum to women although it retained the protective social environment of the academies (Horowitz, 1984, pp. 11–12, 28). Several other college-level institutions for

women followed. Together they are known as the Seven Sisters Colleges and by the early 1900s were well-established liberal arts colleges for women:

1. Mount Holyoke College was founded in 1837 as Mount Holyoke Female Seminary by Mary Lyon in South Hadley, Massachusetts. The name changed to Mount Holyoke College in 1893 (Mount Holyoke, n.d., paras. 1, 2).

2. Vassar College was founded in 1861 by Matthew Vassar in Poughkeepsie, New York (Vassar Admissions, n.d., para. 1).

3. Wellesley College was founded in 1870 by Henry and Pauline Durant in Wellesley, Massachusetts (Wellesley College, n.d., para. 1).

4. Smith College was founded in 1871 through the estate of Sophia Smith in Northampton, Massachusetts (Smith College, n.d.).

5. Harvard Annex was founded in 1879 through the leadership of Elizabeth Cary Agassiz. Through the annex, women could be taught by Harvard faculty. In 1894, the annex became Radcliffe College, but it was not until 1943 that women were allowed into Harvard's classrooms. In 1999, Radcliffe College and Harvard officially and fully merged, creating the Radcliffe Institute for Advanced Study at Harvard (Radcliffe Institute, n.d.).

6. Bryn Mawr College was founded in 1885 through the estate of Joseph W. Taylor in Bryn Mawr, Pennsylvania. Under the leadership of M. Carey Thomas, the college emphasized academic rigor (Bryn Mawr, n.d., paras. 1–6).

Coordinate college

single-sex college affiliated with a single-sex college of the opposite gender

7. Barnard College was founded in 1889 as a **coordinate college** with Columbia University in New York City (Barnard, n.d., para.1).

While these institutions expanded educational access for women, their "commitment to increasing educational opportunities...did not entail a commitment to reducing discrimination according to class, ethnicity, or race" (Thelin, 2004, p. 227). Of the seven, only Wellesley and Smith admitted Black women in the late 1800s. Women also began to attend colleges and universities that had previously admitted only men, although not without significant controversy. There was great concern for women's mental and physical health. Dr. Edward Clarke's *Sex in Education*,

widely read and discussed after its publication in 1873, did not argue that women did not have the right to education. Rather, Clarke argued that if women used up their "limited energy" on studying, they would endanger their "female apparatus," because, while they were capable of learning, they could not "do all this" without suffering from a variety of physical and mental ailments, including hysteria and "derangements of the nervous system" (Clarke, cited in Solomon, 1985, p. 56). As Solomon (1985) notes, "this medical verdict put the stamp of scientific truth on the ancient suspicion that the female brain and body could not survive book learning," for it was not an issue of rights but, rather, what was in the best interests of society (pp. 56–57). Institutions like Vassar, which offered the full liberal arts curriculum, incited concerns that "higher education 'unsexed' women, turning them away from their feminine aspirations and graces to masculine hopes and demeanor" (Horowitz, 1984, p. 29).

Several colleges offered admission to women along with men, the first of which was Oberlin College in Ohio in 1837 yet, even there, women were not allowed to read their commencement parts in public until 1857 (Solomon, 1985, p. 29). In 1870, there were 8 state universities open to women. In order of their acceptance of women, they were: Iowa (1855), Wisconsin (1867), Kansas (1869), Indiana (1869), Minnesota (1869), Missouri (1870), Michigan (1870), and California (1870). Iowa, Kansas, and Minnesota admitted women from their origination (Newcomer, 1959, p. 14). By 1870, women had been admitted to 30.7% of the whole number of colleges including technical schools and women's colleges. The movement toward coeducation was taking root, particularly in the West. A report to the commissioner of education in the early 1870s indicates that about 97 institutions enrolled the majority of women: 5 were in New England, 8 were in the middle of the country, 17 were in the South, and 67 in the West. The movement continued to spread and, by 1900, institutions that admitted women constituted 71.6% of the whole (Woody, 1929, pp. 2:251–252).

Throughout the century, acceptance of women in higher education continued to grow. Between 1870 and 1900, the number of women enrolled in institutions of higher education rose from 11,000 to 85,000 and, as a percentage of all students, from 21% to 36.8%. Although

in 1900 only 2.8% of women 18 to 21 years of age were enrolled, women were in college to stay (Newcomer, 1959, p. 46). Over the course of the 20th century, many state-supported institutions began to admit both men and women. It is important to note that this change occurred over time and that, in fact, many institutions continued to discriminate against women in admissions well into the second half of the 20th century. For example, it was not until 1970 that the University of Virginia admitted first-year women into the College of Arts and Sciences (University of Virginia, n.d., para. 2).

Historically Black Colleges and Universities

Historically Black colleges and universities (HBCUs) are academic institutions whose principal mission was, and remains, the education of Black Americans. Most were established prior to 1964, although several institutions which opened after that year have also been given the HBCU designation by the National Association for Equal Opportunity in Higher Education [NAFEO] (Roebuck & Murty, 1993, p. 3). HBCUs were "born out of the exclusionary and discriminatory laws and practices of the dominant White society" but succeeded in providing many Black youth with an educational opportunity that, perhaps for the first time in their lives, was offered in an "environment free of racial discrimination and tension" (Jackson & Nunn, 2003, p. 3). Just before the Civil War, in 1860, there were approximately 4 million slaves, 92% of whom lived in the South among 8 million of the nation's 27 million Whites (Berlin, cited in Roebuck & Murty, 1993, p. 21). Blacks were restricted from earning a college degree in the South, and found limited opportunities elsewhere. Tennessee was the only southern state that did not legally prohibit the formal instruction of slaves or free Blacks. Over 90% of the South's adult Black population was illiterate (Foner, cited in Roebuck & Murty, 1993, p. 21). Lack of educational preparation and the widespread social custom of segregation throughout the country created significant obstacles to the development of higher education for Black Americans. Still, Black leaders and reform-minded Whites made progress. In the North, the Institute for Colored Youth was established in 1837 through the generosity of Quaker Richard Humphrey in Philadelphia. This institution would later be called Cheyney University of Pennsylvania. Two

early foundations did not survive: Avery College (chartered in 1849) in Allegheny City, Pennsylvania, and Miner Academy (opened in 1851) in Washington, D.C. Ashmun Institute, founded in 1854 by Presbyterians, would become the influential institution known as Lincoln University in Pennsylvania. Wilberforce University was founded in 1856 by Ohio Methodists, but the struggling institution closed, only to be purchased and reopened in 1863 by the African Methodist Episcopal Church. Black colleges in the North included Central State University in Ohio, chartered in 1887 as the "Combined Normal and Industrial Department" of Wilberforce. Eventually, it developed into a separate four-year college. Four of the northern Black colleges that were founded in the 19th century survived into the 20th: Lincoln, Wilberforce, Cheyney, and Central State (Lucas, 2006, p. 164–165; Wilberforce, n.d., paras. 1–3).

Prior to the Civil War, only twenty-eight Black individuals had received a bachelor's degree from a U.S. college or university. Some had attended predominately White institutions that selectively admitted Blacks, such as Berea College in Kentucky and Oberlin College in Ohio but, even at institutions that allowed access, Black students were commonly required to live in segregated housing or off campus. After the Civil War, about 5 million free Blacks lived in the United States and opportunities for advancement were severely limited. The development of a system of education was required to provide basic instruction in reading, writing, and arithmetic. Northern missionary societies took the first steps by sending missionaries to "uplift" the freed slaves and their children through religion, education, and resources. The **American Missionary Association** was responsible for establishing seven Black colleges and thirteen normal schools between 1861 and 1870. Other missionary societies and the **Freedmen's Bureau** followed suit, although they faced tremendous obstacles including a system of laws to disenfranchise Blacks, limits on the growth of Black education, and a preference among the White population for vocational rather than classical education for Blacks. Although mandated by law after 1865 to provide a public school education for all citizens, the system was very slow to develop. Blacks recognized this problem and organized to establish educational opportunities for themselves. They formed societies, raised money, purchased land, built schoolhouses, and paid teachers, so

American Missionary Association

integrated group of Protestant religious leaders who worked for the freedom and advancement of the Black population

Freedmen's Bureau

federal agency created after the Civil War to supervise relief and educational activities of freed slaves

that by 1869, nearly 3,000 schools serving over 150,000 students were in existence in addition to those operated by joint efforts of White missionary societies and Black groups (Roebuck & Murty, 1993, pp. 22–24; Forner, cited in Roebuck & Murty, 1993, p. 25).

More than 200 Black private institutions bearing titles such as "normal," "college," or "university" were founded in the South between 1865 and 1890 with the assistance of northern churches, missionary groups, and the Freedmen's Bureau. Many were largely elementary in nature and did not survive into the 20th century. Still, they paved the way for students to attend and succeed in higher education and some, including Fisk, Howard, Leland, Lincoln, Shaw, and Wilberforce, initiated college departments by or before 1872 (Du Bois & Dill, cited in Roebuck & Murty, 1993, p. 26). Public HBCUs also developed prior to 1890. None initially granted bachelor's degrees and all but two began as normal or industrial schools. Seventeen of the public Black colleges that survived into the 20th century were founded as a consequence of the second Morrill Act of 1890 (Roebuck & Murty, 1993, p. 27). In its original form, the federal act sought to bar land-grant funds from any state where a "distinction of race or color was made"; but, in its final form, a compromise had been reached so that in its language and practical effect states that maintained separate colleges would be required to support programs of "like character" and distribute funds on a "just and equitable" basis. States moved to designate existing Black schools as land-grant recipients and to create new ones. By 1900, all of the southern and border states had government-supported Black colleges. Most, however, did not heed the mandate of the Morrill Act to take mechanical and agricultural arts as their "leading object" and they frequently offered instruction well below even a secondary level (Lucas, 2006, pp. 170–171).

As the century neared its end, a debate over the most appropriate curriculum for Black higher education was given a national stage. W. E. B. Du Bois, born free in 1868 in Massachusetts, graduated from Fisk University and continued to Harvard. He was the first Black man to earn a Harvard Ph.D. As a professor at Atlanta University, he was a scholar, author, activist, and nationally respected Black leader. He held that the highest level of education any man could attain, that offered by a liberal arts curriculum, was

the most appropriate education to develop Black leaders. He supported the idea that if the most talented of the race (the "talented tenth") were properly educated, they would successfully guide the rest. Du Bois advocated for political power, civil rights, and a liberal higher education. Booker T. Washington believed the progress of the race required a different type of training. He was born a slave in Virginia in 1856. Washington attended the Hampton Institute and was the founder of the Tuskegee Institute, both of which offered teacher and vocational training. As a strong proponent of practical education, he sought compromise with southern Whites and believed vocational and industrial education would allow Blacks to become self-sufficient. In Washington's opinion, Whites would come to recognize the practical benefits of industrial training for Blacks and endorse their education. Acceptance of the race would eventually follow. Washington was willing to support the segregated status quo in order to ensure White investment in Black economic development (Jackson & Nunn, 2003, pp. 25–27). Most southern Whites and many others in the majority culture in the North supported Washington's conciliatory view. Others, including Black intellectuals, agreed with Du Bois.

Normal Schools

Intended to describe a place where the "norms" of exemplary teaching practice were shared, the term *normal* was derived "via the French from the Latin *norma*, meaning conforming to a rule, pattern or mode" (Lucas, 2006, p. 139). The first formal attempt to educate men and women specifically for teaching positions in public schools was made in New England in 1838 when the Massachusetts legislature established four state normal schools, the first of which opened for women in Lexington in July 1839. In 1856, enrollment at the four schools totaled no more than 332 students, of whom 290 were women. Those admitted were at least 16 or 17 years old (depending on the school), were required to declare their intention to teach, document their good moral character, and pass an entrance examination. With allowance for minor differences, the year-long curriculum included the "common branches" of learning taught in primary schools, a limited number of secondary academic subjects, child development, methods of teaching and classroom management, and a period of practice in a

model school. In order to earn the teaching certificate, the student was expected to complete the full course. However, even those who did not were likely to be hired elsewhere in the country as the need for teachers was great. The longer, two-year course was adopted in Massachusetts around 1860 (Lucas, 2006, pp. 139–144).

Other states were also actively pursuing the normal school concept. In 1844, the New York state legislature authorized the creation of a normal school that was established in Albany. By 1868, there were eight normal schools in New York including Albany, Oswego, Buffalo, Brockport, Cortland, Potsdam, Fredonia, and Geneseo (Harper, 1939, pp. 48–49). These schools were tuition free and operated under the assumption that the state had an obligation to provide qualified teachers for the public schools. In May 1850, Connecticut opened its first normal school in New Britain with an enrollment of thirty. The citizens of Rhode Island joined the movement with the opening of a state normal school around 1854. The New Jersey State Normal and Model School was established in Trenton in 1855. In Pennsylvania, the first "model school" was established in Philadelphia in 1818, and in 1848 it was reorganized into a normal school. In 1857, Pennsylvania law allowed for the creation of a semiprivate system of normal schools, one for each of the twelve districts of the state (Harper, 1939, pp. 52–66). During the period from 1860 to 1890, the normal schools of the East tended to enroll mostly women to teach at the elementary level. In the West and South as well, male students were the minority (about 26%). Young men who had shown higher academic potential than their classmates would secure teaching certificates, teach for several years in the district schools, and enroll in the normal school with a goal of becoming principals or superintendents in the city schools (Harper, 1939, p. 107).

The normal schools of the West were more influential than their counterparts in the East, largely due to two factors. The public school system in the West was in the process of formation and the normal schools were accorded a prominent role in the development of its plans and policies. Also, there was not a "strongly entrenched" system of secondary and higher education institutions so the pressure to limit the work of normal schools was not as great (Harper, 1939, p. 73).

Across the country, the demand for teachers contin-ued to grow. By 1870, an extensive educational system had been established in the United States with more than 6,871,000 students in public schools, of whom 6,791,000 were at the elementary level. By 1889, twenty-three of the thirty-eight states had state boards of education, and a system of teacher certification by examination had devel-oped. Ninety-two state-supported normal schools were established by 1890, most offering courses of two to three years (Hofstadter & Hardy, 1952, p. 95). By the end of the 19th century, there were almost 130 state normal schools in operation. Still, these graduates accounted for only about 10% to 40% of the teachers entering schools each year. Other educational institutions, including private acade-mies, public secondary schools, and some Latin grammar schools, also continued to prepare individuals who became employed as teachers (Lucas, 2006, p. 144).

There did exist in the East as well as the West a con-tinuing tension between the growing normal school move-ment and the educational establishment embodied in the colleges and universities, particularly as normal schools expanded to a four-year curriculum and began to award degrees. The debate concerned not only what type of insti-tution was best suited to prepare teachers but also what constituted the best education for them, general liberal arts or professional. It was noted that preparing individuals to teach was among the oldest functions of the liberal arts college and the university. Consequently, some educators believed the teachers colleges could appropriately award standard degrees. However, many of the teachers-college leaders felt that the degree offered by the teachers col-leges should be a distinctly professional one. There was no consensus over whether to offer the standard A.B., as the bachelor of arts was known; the relatively newer B.S. (bachelor of science); or the even newer bachelor of educa-tion (Harper, 1939, p. 147). As a result, the degrees and the preparation varied.

Professional Education

During this 1800s, professional education, particu-larly in law and medicine, began to move in a new direc-tion. Most professional men had prepared for careers in law, medicine, or ministry through an apprenticeship. The apprenticeship system required a boy or young man

to work directly under the supervision of a professional man for some unspecified period of time (usually a few months to a few years) during which he would learn and slowly begin to take on the work as his own career. A young apprentice would learn practice and theory by reading extensively from the master's library and, through observation and limited participation, he would learn the customs and nuances of the work. The novice had the advantage of learning by doing; the master enjoyed the benefits of an interested and helpful assistant. Sometimes the master also charged the novice a fee for the opportunity. The system, however, had critical flaws, one of the most important of which was the uneven training apprentices received. Theoretical training was only as thorough as the depth of the master's library, and not all great practitioners were equally gifted teachers. There was little or no opportunity to learn what was new in the profession. This system of apprenticeship was slowly left behind as undergraduate colleges began to offer professionally relevant course work and loosely organized apprenticeship programs developed into the very early professional schools in law and medicine. The schools developed as one lawyer took on a number of apprentices or several doctors banded together to offer apprenticeships to a group of men. This type of arrangement had several significant advantages: (1) they produced a profit for the professional men as they collected and split tuition payments; (2) the masters received some degree of assistance from the apprentices; and (3) the novices were exposed to more than one master or teacher. In the interest of efficiency, these schools moved increasingly toward a lecture method of imparting knowledge rather than allowing students to practice alongside the professional. In time, the lectures formed the textbooks and professional programs were available at established colleges and universities, although a bachelor's degree was not usually required for admission. In fact, it was only after the Civil War that the new president of Harvard College, Charles Eliot, convinced each of the Harvard graduate schools to require a bachelor's degree. Initially enrollment fell, but it did not take long for Harvard's professional school graduates to make a favorable impression and enrollment rose again. This success prompted other institutions to require at least two years of liberal undergraduate

education for admission to professional schools (Brubacher & Rudy, 1976, pp. 200–205).

Catholic Colleges and Universities

Whether supported primarily by private philanthropy or state subsidies, higher education was dominated by various Protestant denominations from the colonial period through the 19th century. The Roman Catholic school system of education fully developed in the 20th century but traces its roots to the first Catholic bishop in the United States. He was John Carroll. Ordained a **Jesuit**, he was a friend of Benjamin Franklin and an advocate for Catholic education. Throughout his travels, Carroll observed the strong Protestant atmosphere that existed in educational institutions. On December 15, 1785, he wrote: "The object nearest my heart now and the only one that can give consistency to our religious views in this country, is the establishment of a school, and afterwards a seminary for young clergy" (Buetow, 1970, p. 49). In his first pastoral letter, dated May 28, 1792, he addressed the subject of education, emphasizing the importance of Catholic education to insure the young grow up in the faith. At that time, there were only about 25,000 Catholics in the United States, very few of whom were educated. Although the number was relatively small, the bishop was keenly aware of the shortage of Catholic priests to serve them as, in 1785, there were only about twenty-four in the country. Through his efforts, and those of other concerned clergy, Georgetown College accepted its first student on November 22, 1791. Twelve years later, in 1803, the second Roman Catholic college, St. Mary's College, was established and opened in Baltimore. Mount St. Mary's College in Emmitsburg, Maryland, followed in 1808 (Buetow, 1970, pp. 45–57).

One of the most significant developments in the history of Catholic higher education was the founding of Catholic University of America. Miss Mary Gwendoline Caldwell of Baltimore offered a sum of $300,000 to the bishops of the Third Plenary Council in 1884 to be used for the establishment of a National Catholic School of Philosophy and Theology. She offered the funds subject to six very specific conditions, several of which dealt with the governance of the institution and included that she be considered the foundress. Although the bishops of the United States are now identified as the founders, instruction began

Jesuit

Catholic priest who is a member of the Society of Jesus

at Catholic University in Washington, D.C., in 1889. All thirty-eight students were in the School of Theology, the only school in operation at the time. The university functioned primarily as a graduate institution until 1904 when undergraduates were formally admitted to all departments except theology (Power, 1958, pp. 223–235).

Before and through the first half of the 19th century, most Catholic colleges were six- or seven-year schools. Usually a combination of secondary and higher education, Catholic colleges were often obliged to provide foundational instruction as well. Edward J. Power (1972) offers rationale for this arrangement rooted in the distrust of sectarian public secondary education and the apparent lack of confidence even in Catholic secondary education. As a result, a student was expected to attend the same Catholic "college" for secondary and higher studies. Transfer between institutions was very difficult. This system became untenable with the standardization of elementary and secondary curriculum in the United States and the advent of accreditation for higher education. Still, change was slow. In their report to the United States Commissioner of Education in 1872, it was clear that the Catholic colleges continued to retain custody of Catholic secondary education. One Catholic college reported that it had organized a two-year college course; 23 offered a four-year course, which included both high school and college studies; 2 had a five-year course; 5 offered a six-year course; and the remaining 20 Catholic colleges either ignored the commissioner's survey or refused to answer. Over time, many of these institutions separated the early years of study into an "academic department" (eventually to become a high school) and a "collegiate department" (destined to become a more traditional college) (Power, 1972, pp. 240–244).

The mass immigration of Catholics from Ireland and Germany between 1833 and 1890 had a significant impact on the development of Catholic education at all levels. Immigration figures indicate that approximately 92,484 individuals came from Ireland to the United States in 1846; 196,224 in 1847; 173,174 in 1848; and 204,771 in 1849. By 1860, the total had reached 1,611,304 (Wittke, cited in Buetow, 1970, p. 112). While the Catholic Church encouraged its immigrant members to adopt American attitudes, these efforts were often painful and not always successful, particularly with the German group during this period

as they often demanded parishes and schools that gave instruction in their native language (Buetow, 1970, p. 114). Many immigrant groups, especially those from eastern Europe who arrived in America during the final decades of the 19th century and the early 20th century, posed a difficult problem as the "preservation of language and culture was of fundamental importance to them" and "the guarantee that they could continue to express their Catholic faith through old-world tradition became an essential goal and it formed the basis of their willingness to adapt to the American Catholic church" (Liptak, 1989, pp. 131–136). As a result, ethnic Catholic parish grammar schools developed that were taught in the native language of the local community and attempted to preserve their traditions.

Nonsectarian religion
Protestant religious orientation without regard to specific denomination

Although Horace Mann's **nonsectarian religion** in the public schools had been generally accepted by the Protestant population, the newly arrived Catholic immigrants saw the common schools as reflecting the "Protestant ethos which permeated American culture" and could not accept the idea of a nonsectarian common school with denominational religious instruction provided at Sunday school. The immigrants and the Catholic Church hierarchy "could not in conscience permit their children to attend schools conducted mainly by Protestant teachers, with a Protestant viewpoint, and with religious instruction and religious exercises of a decidedly Protestant" character (Buetow, 1970, p. 114). The founding of several nativist movements, including the Native American Party (1835), the Know-Nothing Party (1852), and the American Protective Association (1887) along with increasing concern on the part of Protestant citizens that the Catholic Church was subversive to true Americanism exacerbated the situation (Burns, 1937, pp. 107–108). This anti-Catholic bias, the strong Protestant ethos evident in the public system, and the desire on the part of the Catholic church to instruct children in the faith led to the development of an extensive parallel Catholic system of education. Meetings of the Catholic hierarchy in Baltimore resulted in directives to local parishes to establish parochial elementary schools and compelled parents to the support these schools and enroll their children. This was particularly true of the bishops' Third Plenary Council held in 1884. Issues concerning education at all levels were discussed, including elementary and high schools, colleges, and seminaries. The council authored strong decrees directing parish priests to establish and support parish schools as quickly as possible. In 1883, the year preceding the council, there were approximately 6,241 Catholic churches in the country and, of these, 40% (2,491) had schools. By 1913, there were approximately 9,500 churches with resident pastors. Of those parishes, about 5,250 (55%) had schools. Throughout the 1920s, the number of Catholic parishes, schools, teachers, and pupils increased. By 1933, there were 12,537 parishes, of which about 7,462 (60%) had schools (Burns, 1937, pp. 140–144). While these figures do not fulfill the decree of the council that all parishes should establish schools, clearly an increase of 4,971 schools over a fifty-year period (an average of almost 100 per year) was considerable.

While only forty-two Catholic colleges were founded between 1786 and 1849, the development of a system of Catholic education beginning at the elementary level fed the growth of secondary and Catholic colleges throughout the latter half of the 19th century.

Of these first forty-two institutions, 18 owe their origin to the bishop of the diocese (8 of these were transferred to religious communities by 1850), 18 were founded by religious communities or persons representing religious congregations, and 5 were created by secular priests as private-venture institutions but were, by 1850, under the control of the diocese or a religious community. One school, Jefferson College, existed only briefly, and details of its foundation are difficult to ascertain. After 1850, there was a dramatic increase in the development of Catholic colleges as American higher education in general became more necessary socially, politically, and economically. One hundred fifty-two Catholic colleges for men were founded between 1850 and 1900. Ninety-eight of these institutions were established by religious communities, 35 by bishops, 12 by priests, and 2 were developed by laymen as private-venture schools. There is insufficient information available to classify 5 of the colleges founded during these years (Power, 1972, pp. 42–46).

Catholic colleges for women developed nearly a half century after their non-Catholic counterparts (Power 1972, p. 294), the first being the College of Notre Dame of Maryland in 1896 (Cameron, cited in Power, 1972, p. 303). Since Catholic colleges were founded on the assumption that they were created to prepare priests, they ignored "any and

all legitimate demands prospective women students might make on them" and "stood deaf and impervious to justifications for coeducation until the twentieth century was well advanced and, even when it became clear that such restrictive policies deprived women of their educational rights, amendments to them were adopted painfully and reluctantly" (Power, 1972, p. 238). Most Catholic colleges for women began, like their non-Catholic counterparts, as academies. George C. Stewart Jr. (1994) reports that thirty-four Catholic academies or colleges were opened for women by communities of women religious between 1809 and 1899 (pp. 549–550). The School Sisters of Notre Dame became among the first to award the bachelor's degree when they transformed their Baltimore academy into the College of Notre Dame of Maryland in 1896 and granted their first baccalaureate degrees in 1899. Other religious congregations were on a parallel track. Among the Catholic colleges for women founded by the turn of the century were: St. Mary's College in South Bend [now Notre Dame], Indiana (established by the Sisters of the Holy Cross); St. Mary of the Woods College in Terre Haute, Indiana (established by the Sisters of Providence); the College of St. Elizabeth in Convent Station, New Jersey (established by the Sisters of Charity); and the College of New Rochelle in New Rochelle, New York (established by the Ursuline Sisters). In 1900, Trinity College was founded by the Sisters of Notre Dame in Washington, D.C., and was the first to open as a college rather than as an academy (Mahoney, 2002, pp. 25–26).

State Universities

The University of Georgia can lay claim to being the first state university based on its charter date of 1785. However, it did not open and hold classes until 1801. The University of North Carolina received its charter in 1789 but first admitted students in 1795. Although these institutions are among the early state institutions, a number of other colleges and universities in the early 1800s received government support through tax benefits, special levies, or land grants, although the contemporary concept of a "public" educational institution was not yet fully realized. Sometimes these colleges were thought of as "state colleges" but they were not under government control and often maintained strong religious ties with the Protestant sect through which they were founded. During the 1800s,

a new type of institution was established that emphasized a deliberate public and non-religious orientation. According to John S. Brubacher and Willis Rudy (1976), the founders of these new institutions were influenced by the European Enlightenment, the French and American revolutions, and the idea that applied knowledge should be used to improve the human condition. It became apparent when established institutions did not respond enthusiastically to this new concept that the state would have to step in more directly. The Enlightenment and the Revolutionary periods helped to form the "belief that by taking proper governmental action social institutions could be remodeled to a more just order. The classical tradition in higher education was seen, from this point of view, as nothing but a decadent scholasticism.... In the new age of American independence and republicanism, education of the highest sort should be broadly disseminated.... And it should be free of religious sects" (pp. 144–145).

While it cannot claim to be the first state university based on the date of its charter, the University of Virginia (1819) is considered by some scholars to be the first university that truly embodied the elements of the modern state university. From the beginning, it aimed to be free of religious domination and to offer more advanced instruction than what was available at most existing colleges at the time. The university offered elective options to students, and the state of Virginia invested in the original buildings, library, and equipment and continued to give an annual appropriation to support its work. Thomas Jefferson is considered the founder of the university based on the depth and significance of his ideas and his extraordinary influence on its creation. Under his guidance, eight professorships were established covering study in ancient languages, modern languages, mathematics, natural philosophy, natural history, anatomy and medicine, moral philosophy, and law (Brubacher & Rudy, 1976, pp. 147–151). Jefferson hoped the university would become an institution "in which all the branches of science useful *to us*, and *at this day* should be taught in their highest degree" (emphasis is his). He recommended the study of agriculture, natural sciences, civil history, and law on account of their utility (Boorstin, cited in Brubacher & Rudy, 1976, p. 151). Jefferson's ideas were emulated in pockets of the country by forward-thinking

individuals who recognized their value in sustaining a strong democracy.

Research Universities, Graduate Institutions, and Technical Schools

Historian Frederick Rudolph (1962) identified several key issues that affected colleges during the 19th century and prompted change. One was the election of Andrew Jackson as the seventh president of the United States in 1828. Jackson embodied the common man whom he so well represented, hard work over privilege, respect for labor, and faith in the people. The belief that "unless an institution served all men equally, it served America poorly" found its way into the college debate (p. 203). The value of the classical curriculum was questioned as it generally lacked practical application and would be of little value in building a nation. Another key issue was the growth of the sciences. Science had been accepted as a way to understand nature and thus glorify God. As the investigative sciences (with experiments, laboratories, specimen collections, and equipment) began to grow, the sciences came to be viewed in terms of what they could offer man to improve his life in this world. As early as 1727, Harvard appointed a professor of mathematics and natural philosophy. In 1802, Benjamin Silliman was appointed professor of chemistry and natural history at Yale. A Yale graduate himself, he had visited the Princeton laboratory of the first American chemistry professor, John MacLean. By the mid-18th century, the subjects of mathematics, natural philosophy, botany, chemistry, zoology, geology, and mineralogy were available in most colleges, although they did not command the attention of the classical curriculum and were sometimes available only as electives. While the B.A. remained valued and protected, both Harvard and Yale adopted a new degree for their scientific students. Harvard offered its first bachelor of science (B.S.) in 1851; Yale offered the bachelor of philosophy in 1852. The scientific students were admitted with lower requirements than the B.A. candidates, studied for three years rather than four, and were often treated like second-class citizens, but they had arrived (Rudolph, 1962, pp. 221–232).

It is important to note that a universal definition of a *research university* did not exist in America as these institutions first developed. The term has come to mean "an edu-

cational institution of large size which affords instruction of an advanced nature in all the main branches of learning" (Brubacher & Rudy, 1976, p. 143). As they developed, however, they were certainly not large, the constantly changing level of advanced study was relative, and many did not include study in all branches of learning. Advanced study and research activity developed through the influence brought to bear by young American scientists who had studied in Germany. "Between 1820 and 1920, almost 9,000 Americans studied at German universities, the majority during the last decades of the 19th century" and most earning a German Ph.D. (Gruber, 1975, p. 17). The peak of American study in Germany was 1895–96, when 517 were matriculated at German institutions. The German academic ideals of **Lehrfreiheit** and **Wissenschaft** played a significant role in American understanding of the academic enterprise. *Lehrfreiheit,* the freedom to investigate and teach, protected non-utilitarian learning, or **pure research**. *Wissenschaft* refers to research and writing, generally, as opposed to teaching. A third value, that of **Lernfreiheit**, or the freedom of the student to learn, made its way into the American experience through the allowance for course election by students (Veysey, 1965, pp. 126–130). American research institutions tended to support both **applied research** and pure research, stressing one or the other depending on the mission of the institution and the source of its financial support.

Universities were created in a variety of ways: some grew from existing private institutions that added graduate studies and hired faculty with an interest in research; others were the product of legislative fiat at the state level (state universities); some were created through the financial support of the federal government (land grants); some, like Cornell University, were the product of public and private cooperation; and a few were founded as private universities through an endowment. A handful in this final category had the good fortune to rise up through the generosity of a single substantial endowment (Hofstadter & Hardy, 1952, pp. 31–32). Through the course of the century, leaders in various parts of the country attempted to create universities that would meet the needs of a particular region. Challenges included financial problems, denominational hostility, lack of qualified faculty and proper equip-

---

Lehrfreiheit

German, meaning freedom of the professor to investigate and teach the results of his/her research without governmental interference

---

Wissenschaft

German, meaning scholarly research and writing

Pure research

research for the value of discovery

Lernfreiheit

German, meaning freedom of the student to choose his/her own studies in an elective system

---

Applied research

research with the intention of solving a problem

ment, and poor secondary training of potential students (Brubacher & Rudy, 1976, pp. 148–156).

A focus on research dominated Johns Hopkins University, which was founded in 1876 as the first graduate-only institution in the United States. The founding president, Daniel C. Gilman, was intent on spending the Hopkins bequest on the acquisition of the strongest scholars he could recruit. Gilman was determined to create "a nonsectarian institution dedicated to the unfettered search for truth" (Brubacher & Rudy, 1976, p. 179). Following Hopkins' lead, three new institutions were founded as universities with a graduate orientation: Clark University (1888) in Worcester, Massachusetts, with G. Stanley Hall as president; Catholic University of America (1889) with Bishop John J. Keane as rector; and the University of Chicago (1890) with William Rainey Harper as president. The institution in Chicago was the most innovative, as it was the combination of two older foundations and, for the first time, organized the academic structure to include five divisions: "the University Proper; the University Extension; the University Press; the University Laboratories, Libraries, and Museums; and the Affiliations." The financial support of Chicago businessmen and the tremendous financial commitment of outsider John D. Rockefeller Sr. allowed Harper to establish a "great university" with a faculty of 120 prepared to offer advanced work in all of twenty-seven subject-matter fields to the enrolled student body of 594 (Brubacher & Rudy, 1976, pp. 185–186).

An emphasis on science was also evident in the development of technical schools, a number of which opened in the first half of the 19th century. Some of these institutions trained the faculty who would later carry scientific instruction more broadly into the mainstream. One of the earliest and most successful was the Rensselaer School, which was founded in 1824 by Stephen Van Rensselaer and became Rensselaer Polytechnic Institute in 1861. In the founding document, Van Rensselaer envisioned a school

> for the purpose of instructing persons, who may choose to apply themselves, in the application of science to the common purposes of life. My principal object is, to qualify teachers for instructing the sons and daughters of farmers and mechanics by lectures or otherwise, in the application of experimental chemistry, philosophy, and natural history, to agriculture, domestic economy, the arts, and manufactures.... I am inclined to believe that competent instructors

may be produced in the school at Troy who will be highly useful to the community in the diffusion of a very useful kind of knowledge, with its application to the business of living. (Van Rensselaer, 1824, para. 1)

The federal government also understood the importance of science to national security. The U.S. Military Academy at West Point was established in 1802 to study the arts and science of warfare. The site, on the west bank of the Hudson River, was considered by General George Washington to be the most important strategic position in America during the Revolutionary War, and he had commissioned the fortifications there in 1778. When President Thomas Jefferson later signed legislation to create a military academy on the site, he did so at the urging of soldiers and legislators, including Washington, Alexander Hamilton, and John Adams, who wished to eliminate the U.S. reliance on foreign engineers and artillerists (United States Military Academy, n.d., paras. 1–3).

Land-Grant Colleges

The value of scientific study and utility in the curriculum found a number of champions, among them Congressman Justin Smith Morrill from Vermont. The idea of offering a grant of land to support education was a familiar concept by the mid-1800s. Each state west of the Appalachian Mountains that joined the union after 1804 was granted two townships for the creation of an institution of learning. By mid-century, over 4 million acres of public land had been donated in this way for this purpose. The Land Grant College Act (popularly known as the Morrill Act) was signed into law by President Abraham Lincoln in 1862. Although its impact had far-reaching effects, some scholars maintain that, contrary to some traditional accounts, there was little enthusiasm for the opportunities it presented at the time (Lucas, 2006, pp. 155–158). The act proposed to establish colleges where the teaching of agriculture, mechanics, and military tactics was required, where the liberal studies were not omitted, and where other areas could be included as desired by the states (Eddy, 1957, p. 52). In 1867, Morrill offered his own summary:

The bill proposed to establish at least one college in every State upon a sure and perpetual foundation, accessible to all, but especially to the sons of toil, where all the needful science for the practical applications of life shall be taught,

where neither the higher graces of classical studies, nor that military drill our country now so greatly appreciates, will be entirely ignored, and where agriculture, the foundation of all present and future prosperity, may look for troops of earnest friends, studying its familiar and recondite economies, at last elevating it to that higher level, where it may fearlessly invoke comparison with the most advanced standards of the world. The bill fixes the leading objects, but properly, as I think, leaves to the States considerable latitude in carrying out the practical details. (*The North American Review*, cited in Eddy, 1957, p. 34)

Morrill's reference to the practical details included acceptance of the act's terms by the states, decisions on where the land-grant colleges should be located, what their curriculum should be, and the development of state-specific plans to use the land to generate a revenue stream for the institution(s) within each state. Edward D. Eddy (1957) notes that the distribution of the 17,430,000 acres of land broke with precedent in that they were distributed according to the population, assuming the greater the population the greater the need (p. 36). The act provided every state with 30,000 acres of public land for each senator and congressman to which it was entitled by the apportionment of 1860. Every state was expected to establish at least one college within five years or risk forfeiting the proceeds it had acquired from the land to date. These land grants were not gifts of land on which a state government could build a college but, rather:

> the Act established a complex partnership in which the federal government would provide incentives for each state to sell distant western lands, with the states being obliged to use the proceeds to fund advanced instructional programs.... The state government was then required to dedicate the land sale proceeds to establish collegiate programs in such "useful arts" as agriculture, mechanics, mining, and military instruction hence, the "A & M" in the name of many land-grant colleges. (Thelin, 2004, p. 76)

The funds from the sale of the land were to be safely invested and only the interest used to support the colleges. According to Eddy (1957), states followed a variety of organizational patterns in the establishment of the land-grant colleges. Some assigned the funds to a private or church-related college, some to a state university, and some used the funds to create a new and separate institution (p. 49).

In 1890, the second Morrill Act provided annual expenditures for the land-grant colleges and set an important restriction in place: no money would go to states that denied education to individuals because of race. However, segregated ("separate but equal") institutions were allowed. The 1890 act also allowed the "federal monetary grant to be withheld in the case of any state which failed...to maintain in its institution the standards set by federal law" and more narrowly defined the subject matter that federal funds would support (Brubacher & Rudy, 1976, p. 229). Even with the new restrictions, additional land-grant colleges were created. A total of 69 were founded as a result of the Morrill acts of 1862 and 1890 (List of the 107, 1997, p. 363). Although some of these colleges have developed international reputations, most struggled to sustain themselves and to attract enrollment during their formative years. This was due, in part, to the fact that the educational system had not developed sufficiently at the elementary and secondary levels to produce sufficient numbers of college-ready students. As a result, many colleges included those students in preparatory programs in their enrollment figures. Even so, Eldon J. Johnson (1981) offers a bleak picture based on college histories and public data:

> In New Hampshire, literally no new student showed up for the fall opening in 1877. Missouri had the same experience during the first week of the opening term in 1866, although 40 did appear later. Pennsylvania's opening "capacity attendance" had dropped to 22 in 1869 and then took almost 30 years to reach 150. Massachusetts had drastic ups and downs, with 20 years required to get the enrollment back to the modest 1870 level. Neighboring Connecticut opened in 1881 with 12 "on the ground or on the way." In its first 20 years, Nevada never exceeded 35. A decade after the Civil War, no fewer than five institutions in Baltimore had "an enrollment at least double that of the little farmer's College" (University of Maryland), which in eight postwar years had five presidents, under whom six students actually were graduated. Florida's college had a particularly difficult time: the 38 who began in 1884 were all in the preparatory department, and only 57 were in collegiate classes as late as 1898. (p. 337)

Faculty and Governance

Governing boards were in control of institutions during this period. In the early years, they were generally com-

posed of clergymen but later became more secular in nature. Rudolph (1962) notes that as more and more non-alumni faculty were hired, the governing boards began to see them as invaders. The faculty were allowed to tend to the curriculum and college management, but the decisions concerning the mission of the college and its public image were matters left to the board. By the end of the 19th century, boards of trustees were increasingly composed of men with business savvy, political power, and the means to influence the direction of the institution with their personal financial support. The endowed support of professorships could move an institution toward a more scientific orientation or, in a few spectacular cases, establish entire institutions in a model supported by the founder as was the case at Cornell (1865), Johns Hopkins (1876), Stanford (1891), and the University of Chicago (1892).

As the century progressed, the role of the president changed from that of a live-in professor who personally knew and taught most students to one who increasingly became the spokesman for the board. Boards composed primarily of businessmen had limited time for direct management and delegated much of their authority to the president. During this period, the "clergyman president" was slowly discarded because, according to Rudolph (1962), "he...lacked skill in the ways of the world, because his commitment to the classical curriculum stood in the way of the more practical and popular emphasis which commended itself to the trustees, and because the world in which the colleges and universities now moved was secular, less subject to religious influences" (p. 419). The new college president was a man in and of the world, able to solicit investment from wealthy benefactors and lead the faculty through years of great change.

While institutions diversified and grew away from the foundational support of a particular religious group, faculty roles changed significantly as well. The colonial model of one or two professors, a teaching president, and a group of tutors to instruct and watch over the students gave way to the beginnings of an academic profession during the latter part of the 18th century. During the first quarter of the 19th century, several developments contributed to the creation of a more substantial, permanent faculty. The first was growth, both in the size of individual faculties at established institutions like Yale and Harvard and also in

the founding of new colleges throughout the country. The second was the increasing general acceptance of the professorship as a legitimate career. The third may be changes to the ministerial career. Once a lifetime vocation, ministers were experiencing increased job insecurity and low wages in small town and rural parishes (Finkelstein, 1983). As a consequence of these circumstances, a growing number opted for a professorship rather than a parish.

By 1825, professors outnumbered tutors by a 3-to-1 ratio. During this period of change, faculty members studying in Germany or earning a Ph.D. there returned with discipline-specific knowledge and an appreciation of research. The development of scholarly publications and associations promoted academic inquiry and the dissemination of findings through publication (Cohen, 1998, pp. 70–73). As the 19th century progressed, a growing proportion of faculty members identified the professorship as their primary career, as opposed to the ministry, law, or medicine, and a growing number began their academic career immediately after training for it. During the second half of the century, professors began to be viewed as experts and were called on to serve external roles as public lecturers, writers, and public servants. Steps in the academic career ladder developed. As many as one-third of the Harvard faculty held the position of "instructorship" in 1821 and assistant professors were in place at several institutions by mid-century. These appointments marked the beginning of the end of the role of the tutor. Instructors and assistant professors were likely to be trained specialists and were appointed to a particular department. They were set on a career path that afforded the opportunity for promotion to full professor (Finkelstein, 1983).

The rise of graduate institutions and research universities during the final two decades of the 19th century accelerated the process of professionalization. When William Rainer Harper opened the University of Chicago with an endowment from John D. Rockefeller and other Chicago leaders, he set about recruiting the best professors from other leading institutions and, for some, doubling their salaries. The expectation that all faculty should be both teachers and scholars spread, although as original research increased in importance, faculty enthusiasm for teaching often declined. Academic departments formed, providing support for scholarly activities and a base of

strength and identity within the institution. Academic organizations outside the institution also developed bringing together disciplinary specialists from across the country to discuss scholarship and question and review each other's work. The American Philological Association formed in 1869, the American Historical Association and the Modern Language Association formed in the 1880s, and in the 1890s, the American Chemical Association and the American Psychological Association were established (Cohen, 1998, pp. 124–130). These associations supported the continuing advancement of knowledge and led to the expectation of successful peer review as a prerequisite for tenure in the 20th century.

Student Life

In 1870, there were approximately 67,350 men in colleges and universities plus a small number of women. Total enrollment reached 156,756 by 1890 and, by 1910, it grew to 355,215. The establishment of a standardized secondary education system, the generation of extraordinary wealth, the admission of women and minority group members, the needs of industry, and an appreciation for the usefulness of a college or university education all contributed to enrollment growth (Hofstadter & Hardy, 1952, p. 31).

Rudolph (1962) observes that early in the century, regardless of the "intensity of their denominationalism or the sincerity of their nonsectarianism," colleges developed "suitable agencies of religious life, relationships and organizations and customs, that would help define the American college in this era as a religiously oriented institution" (p. 74). The literary and religious societies of the colonial period survived well and expanded into the 19th century. During the first third of the century, student religious groups formed with varied purposes. Some, such as the Saturday Evening Religious Society at Harvard in 1802, were created to promote the "growth of practical and experimental religion"; some to form a "bond of union and sympathy between Christian men in college" through comparing data and information even to the point of examining religious beliefs and collecting religious artifacts from foreign lands (the Theological Society of Amherst in 1821); and others (Princeton) to share prayer that sometimes resulted in a religious revival (Sheldon, 1901, pp. 158–159). The religious revivals of the early and mid-1800s

offered an outlet for student enthusiasm and an antidote to the indifference or outright animosity students felt toward organized religion. After 1850, a number of institutions abolished compulsory religious services and substituted voluntary ones. The last great revival year was 1858, just before the Civil War.

The literary and religious societies were eventually replaced by Greek letter fraternities which were more social in nature and valued the characteristics of the successful man of this world at the expense of Christian virtues. Asa Tilton observed that the "Civil War, athletics, fraternities, new and varied courses, the elective system, the university plan, the influence of big business and science" in addition to the "change in national ideals, intellectual interests, and educational purposes" all contributed to the end of the literary and debating societies (Tilton, cited in Potter, 1944, p. 93). Fraternities offered an attractive escape from the "monotony, dreariness, and unpleasantness of college life," as they "institutionalized various escapes—drinking, smoking, card playing, singing, and seducing" that had long been an informal part of the college culture (Rudolph, 1962, pp. 146–150).

Slowly, athletics also developed as an outlet for student energy. American students engaged in bowling, boxing, shinny, dancing, marbles, hunting, fishing, wrestling, and more. The arrival of the German *Turnvereine* with the immigrants in the middle of the century stimulated much interest and, by 1853, there were at least sixty German-style gymnastic clubs in America. College students pressed for gymnasiums and, by 1860, such facilities were in operation at the University of Virginia, Harvard, Yale, Amherst, Williams, Bowdoin, and Oberlin. In 1860, Amherst established the Department of Hygiene and Physical Education to care for the health of the undergraduates. To insure that the new activity kept with the traditional spirit, the new gym at Amherst carried the motto: "Keep thyself pure: The body is the temple of the Holy Ghost." In 1852, the first intercollegiate contest of any kind was held; it was a boat race between Yale and Harvard. In 1859, Amherst and Williams played the first game of intercollegiate baseball (Rudolph, 1962, pp. 152–154).

Athletic expression was popular throughout the 19th century but it was football that captured the heart of the American campus. The inaugural American football game,

between Princeton and Rutgers in 1869, imitated the English tradition of play and was primarily a kicking game. Initially at Harvard, then at Yale, the game shifted over the next decade to a running style more in line with English rugby. Since there were no eligibility requirements, players were often traveling professionals. The University of Oregon football team opposed the same men in three successive games against three different colleges. Imagine the reaction of the faculty at Miami University in Ohio when the president "all but required" them to go out for the team (Rudolph, 1962, pp. 373–381).

Early organizations such as the Intercollegiate Football Association formed by Yale, Harvard, Princeton, and Columbia and the American Football Rules Committee made minor revisions in the game and attempted to establish rules to make the game safer, but they were ineffective. Meanwhile, the game became increasingly popular on campus where 120 schools fielded teams in the 1890s, but the press and the public generally continued to decry the brutality of the sport and call for changes. Mass momentum plays like the flying wedge, first used by Harvard against Yale in 1892, produced more injuries than any previous formation (Falla, 1981, pp. 11–15). Real progress toward regulation would begin early in the 20th century.

GLOSSARY

Civil War: war between the American states from 1861 to 1865

Liberal arts: originally included grammar, dialectic, rhetoric, arithmetic, geometry, music, and astronomy

Compulsory Education Law: law requiring school attendance, first passed in 1852 in Massachusetts

Preparatory departments: remedial instruction, offered in college, to prepare students for college-level studies

Legal precedent: legal principle, decided by a court, which provides authority that other courts may follow

Contract clause: Article 1, section 10, clause 1 of the U.S. Constitution prohibits states from enacting any law impairing the obligation of contracts

Normal school: designed to prepare teachers for the public school system

Coordinate college: single-sex college affiliated with a single-sex college of the opposite gender

American Missionary Association: integrated group of Protestant religious leaders who worked for the freedom and advancement of the Black population

Freedmen's Bureau: federal agency created after the Civil War to supervise relief and educational activities of freed slaves

Jesuit: Catholic priest who is a member of the Society of Jesus

Nonsectarian religion: Protestant religious orientation without regard to specific denomination

Lehrfreiheit: German, meaning freedom of the professor to investigate and teach the results of his/her research without governmental interference

Wissenschaft: German, meaning scholarly research and writing

Pure research: research for the value of discovery

Lernfreiheit: German, meaning freedom of the student to choose his/her own studies in an elective system

Applied research: research with the intention of solving a problem

CHAPTER FOUR

Expansion of Higher Education, 1900–1960

Introduction

The 20th century arrived to a nation that had completed a transcontinental railroad and was just beginning to understand the potential of hydroelectric power. Expansion and industrialization brought tremendous wealth to some but exploited many, leaving them in poverty and hopelessness. During the Progressive Era of the late 19th and early 20th centuries, myriad efforts sought to improve American society, raise the standard of living for the disadvantaged and the poor, clean up politics, regulate housing and industry, and limit child labor. Investigative journalists known as muckrakers wrote articles that often shocked the public. Newspapers exposed the horrors of child labor, racial bias, the desperation of people living in slums, political corruption, unhealthy food and drugs, and unfair business practices. Women fought for the right to vote, and reformers worked for improvement in living conditions for the poor, for regulation of alcohol, and for the rights of farmers. It was a time of great change, and the movement toward fairness and inclusion affected higher education as well as other parts of the social fabric. At the same time, the world went to war. World War I was fought between 1914 and

1918 and was followed, on October 29, 1929, by the stock market crash that set in motion an economic depression that was worldwide in scope. The **Great Depression** had a devastating impact on personal income, tax revenue, and international trade.

By 1939, much of the world was at war again. The United States entered the conflict on December 8, 1941, following the bombing of Pearl Harbor. Thousands of men and women enlisted in the military and the economy was revived as new jobs were created to support the war effort. By the end of the war in 1945, America had developed weapons of mass destruction, the world had witnessed their devastating power, and all understood the potential impact of their widespread deployment. The United States, the Soviet Union, and their respective allies warily confronted and competed with each other throughout the long period known as the Cold War. In 1957, the Soviet Union launched Sputnik, the first unmanned spacecraft to orbit the Earth, and set the "space race" in motion. The need for American scientists, engineers, and researchers required a larger, stronger, more advanced and technically oriented educational system. The federal government, while not directly responsible for education in the states, accelerated this transformation with the infusion of financial assistance for research, students, and facilities.

Great Depression
economic collapse that began in October 1929 and lasted about a decade

Evolution of Established Institutions

Standards varied greatly, prompting scholar Laurence R. Veysey (1965) to note that of the 500 institutions of higher learning in 1903, a majority may not even have deserved the title "college," only 100 or so held to standards that would have allowed a graduate to go right on to the doctorate, and only about 12 were universities of the first rank. At Princeton, a master's degree would be awarded to any graduate who submitted a thesis of approximately twenty pages (p. 359). Still, colleges that offered a classical education continued alongside those with a science orientation and, in many cases, individual institutions tried to incorporate both. Over the course of the century, the development of standards for admission and matriculation, articulation with high school programs, accreditation, research, massive enrollment expansion, curriculum diversification, federal funding, science, and technology transformed American higher education dramatically. The

various institutional types established in the 19th century continued into the early 20th although, by the end of the period, some had disappeared and others changed significantly to meet new demands. Many of the traditional liberal arts colleges grew into **comprehensive colleges** during the 20th century, incorporating majors in business and science, in addition to graduate degree programs. Some adopted a research orientation and became research universities. A minority added contemporary new majors but retained their original focus and entered the 21st century as selective liberal arts undergraduate colleges.

Comprehensive colleges
Post-secondary institutions that offer bachelor's and master's degree programs

Colleges for women continued to develop and grow even as coeducation became more popular. While many debated what type of education was the best and most appropriate for women, women themselves were answering the question through their enrollment choices. Women enrolled in academic programs that, in previous generations, would have rejected them. Their success in classical studies and fields such as mathematics, science, medicine, and law continued to challenge the notion that women were mentally or physically incapable of higher learning. Of course, an education was no guarantee of professional acceptance and the usefulness of preparing women for careers that were generally closed to them was argued. Gradually, over the course of the century, women attended classes side by side with men, eventually succeeding in all varieties of occupations and professions.

Education for Black Americans in the early part of the 20th century was divided between education designed to prepare individuals for a vocation and that which would offer preparation for leadership. The mission societies and Black religious organizations responsible for the latter aimed to produce liberally educated men who could lead the race and, as doctors, lawyers, and intellectuals, support its members in a segregated society. Given the deficit of educational preparation for Blacks prior to the Civil War, they faced an enormous challenge. In 1900, in a population of nearly 10 million Blacks, "there were 3,880 Black students in colleges and professional schools and fewer than 400 graduates of colleges and professional programs" (Anderson, 1988, p. 245). Even when added to the 3,000 existing graduates, this was not nearly enough educated men to serve the segregated population. By 1910, "less than one-third of 1% of college-age Blacks were attend-

ing college compared with more than 5% among Whites" (p. 245). Many educational institutions for Blacks were impoverished by the early years of the 20th century and, as accreditation moved forward, they were hard-pressed to survive.

The Hampton-Tuskegee model of **industrial education** to prepare Blacks for vocational employment enjoyed the benefits of industrial philanthropy. Although they also supported a limited number of traditional colleges for Blacks, foundations including the General Education Board, the Phelps-Stokes Fund, the Anna T. Jeanes Foundation, and the Carnegie Foundation all cooperated in support of the industrial model and viewed the "missionary program of Black higher education as the futile and even dangerous work of misguided romantics" (Anderson, 1988, p. 247). It was eventually the liberally educated Black American men who, after World War I, around 1920, began to push hard for social, economic, and educational equality (pp. 260–278).

Throughout the latter half of the 20th century, historically Black colleges and universities continued to offer high-quality education to Blacks, preparing graduates for leadership and professional roles. Reports indicate that, in 1984, two HBCUs accounted for 40% of all Blacks earning degrees in dentistry, two accounted for 22% of all Black medical doctors, four accounted for 16% of all Blacks earning law degrees, and one accounted for 82% of all Black veterinarians. These institutions advocated for equal opportunity while continuing to provide higher education for many who would not otherwise have graduated from college. In time, they also became centers for Black culture and some have established archives to conserve the history of Black Americans (NAFEO, Vol. II, 1991 Report, cited in Roebuck & Murty, 1993, p. 4).

During the first four decades of the 20th century, normal schools continued to gain in popularity and experienced corresponding expansion in enrollment, academic programs, financial support, and influence. Young women in their late teens, like Marcella Scanlon, left rural family farms to enroll with the hope of securing a teaching position (personal communication, July 1980). For many, this was a valuable opportunity to gain personal and financial independence and was especially important for those who did not marry. By 1939, the 150 institutions belonging to

Industrial education
programs designed specifically to prepare an individual for a vocation

the American Association of Teachers Colleges annually enrolled over 180,000 students and furnished about 56% of the public school teachers in the country. Thirty-one of these institutions offered a master's degree. They universally required a high school diploma for admission. The majority of the programs were four years in length and designed to prepare individuals for a wide range of teaching positions including those in the "manual arts, commercial subjects, household economy, kindergarten, primary, lower grades, upper grades, all high school subjects, speech, agriculture, and the like" (Harper, 1939, pp. 152–154). Although many in the normal school movement wished to retain the distinctive character of their institutions, as the normal schools evolved into state teachers colleges during the 20th century and earned the right to confer degrees, the curriculum gradually included more courses in the liberal studies. Conversely, as teacher preparation programs at traditional colleges and universities were established they included more courses specifically designed to prepare teachers for the classroom, including courses in educational methods.

University-level schools of education, concentrating more on research than teacher preparation, also began to appear. They sought to develop a research foundation on which to build and improve elementary and secondary education. William R. Johnson (1989) notes that one of the first and most influential was the Teachers College of Columbia University. Focused on graduate training for educational leaders, the four-year undergraduate course in the School of Practical Arts was eliminated in 1925. This movement was applauded by those who believed a scientific approach to education would solve its problems. Others, including Dean Henry W. Holmes at Harvard, expressed concern that this research approach created a hierarchy which placed university professors and their research orientation above teachers in the schools. As education professors worked to establish academic credentials, their research became more sophisticated and less and less accessible to teachers. Still, no overarching theory of education was developed that addressed the many issues and challenges of 20th-century education in the United States (pp. 242–245). According to Johnson, "the history of twentieth-century teacher training can be seen as a series of institutional displacements, with normal schools

becoming state teachers colleges, then multi-purpose liberal arts colleges, and…, in many instances regional state universities" (p. 243).

Education for the professions also experienced dramatic changes in the 20th century. Brubacher and Rudy (1976) report that, by 1900, "the percentage of people with no training beyond secondary school was rapidly falling. Indeed better than 10% of lawyers, doctors, clergymen, and college teachers…had both college and professional or graduate instruction in preparation for their careers" (p. 204). Within the first twenty-five years of the 20th century, the better professional schools were able to be selective in admission, requiring not only a bachelor's degree but in some cases giving preference to those who had completed certain course work. As liberal arts institutions increasingly created graduate departments, the benefits of tying undergraduate education to graduate education became clearer. Medical students studied biology, chemistry, and psychology as undergraduates; law students studied history, philosophy, and so on. This alignment between undergraduate and graduate education affected the proprietary schools operated by lawyers and doctors. As a result, many either closed or affiliated themselves with established undergraduate colleges and the "teaching" doctors and lawyers became full-time faculty. Lecturing and practice were purposively combined. Medical students practiced in laboratories and hospitals as part of their graduate program experience, thus creating medical internships out of what had once been apprenticeships (Brubacher & Rudy, 1976, pp. 204–208).

Upgrading and regulating the professions continued through the efforts of state examining authorities, associations of practitioners, and associations of professional schools. By 1915, membership in the American Association of Law Schools required a library of at least 5,000 volumes, a minimum of three full-time professors on the faculty, and a minimum three-year term of instruction. Professional associations like the American Bar Association and the American Medical Association along with philanthropic organizations such as the Carnegie Foundation for the Advancement of Teaching began to publish information about the conditions at poor, independent law and medical schools, causing many of them to close. One of the most famous of these studies was undertaken by the Carnegie

Foundation to evaluate medical education. Written by Abraham Flexner and published in 1910, the report was highly critical of many schools. Flexner's intention was to establish the Johns Hopkins University medical program as the standard. Within approximately two years of the report, about 30% of the nation's medical schools had closed, many because they lacked the financial resources to invest in equipment, research, laboratories, and faculty (Thelin, 2004, pp. 148–149). A significant number could not face the negative publicity and closed. In 1890, there were 160 medical schools; thirty years later, in 1920, there were only 85, of which 70 held the highest rating of the American Medical Association (AMA) (Brubacher & Rudy, 1976, pp. 206–207). Although no other profession experienced as dramatic and swift a change as that generated by the Flexner Report, over the course of the century the development of standards for the professions, and their enforcement through state agencies and professional associations, continued to increase academic expectations and raise standards in virtually every profession. Other professional associations also began publishing lists of accredited schools, including the Dental Association in 1918 and the American Bar Association in 1923 (Sanders, 1959, p. 11).

In the late 19th and early 20th centuries, pressure to standardize curriculum and academic requirements reached Catholic colleges as well. Following the lead of St. Louis University, a Jesuit institution, the colleges gradually adopted the St. Louis Plan which separated the high school program from the college program. Reaching further than its intended audience of Jesuit schools, the plan influenced many Catholic colleges. The titles "Humanities, Poetry, Rhetoric, and Philosophy for the four college years" were adopted to correspond to the terms "freshman, sophomore, junior, and senior" at non-Catholic institutions (Power, 1972, p. 246). However, significant curricular change beyond the titles was not forthcoming at Catholic colleges early in the century and they continued to teach a highly proscribed classical curriculum. Although, as Power notes, while the institutions maintained a "theoretical adherence to classical education" they "were seldom capable of fulfilling their advertised expectations" (p. 247). Students also presented challenges to the old order, as the long-revered curriculum "failed the pragmatic test of utility" (p. 247). While appropriate for

the seminary and priesthood, the secular-minded students who arrived on campus during the first several decades of the century were also interested in science and in a college education that would prepare them for professional lives. Some Catholic colleges responded by adjusting the single curriculum to incorporate science, others developed alternative academic tracks that, in addition to the classical, might include the scientific, the commercial, and the pre-divinity courses of study.

Standardization forced many religious communities of men and women to reexamine the goals and methods of higher education in their U.S. institutions. As the century progressed, one of the primary concerns of *non-accredited* institutions, whether Catholic or not, was that their graduates would be denied admission to the highest-quality graduate programs, which were offered at *accredited* colleges and universities. The desire on the part of Catholic colleges to hire Catholic faculty and the requirement on the part of accrediting bodies that faculty members have higher degrees (master's and doctorates) intensified the problem. Although similar issues were being experienced throughout the country, the example of the Jesuits and the North Central Association of Colleges and Secondary Schools (NCA) provides a descriptive case. By 1773, the Jesuits were operating over 800 educational institutions worldwide (Mahoney, 2003, p. 42) and, so, brought significant expertise and experience to the effort to establish colleges in the United States. They also brought a strong and well-tested plan for education in the *Ratio Studiorum*, their long-standing pedagogical model outlining the matter, aims, and methods of education. Revised in 1832, it was similar in some respects to the classical curriculum of the early non-Catholic colleges. It required Greek, rhetoric, grammar, philosophy, and the humanities and sought to connect an understanding of the world to God's plan for it from a Catholic perspective. Lester F. Goodchild (1986) has studied the controversy between the NCA and the Jesuit institutions of the Midwest and Chicago regions and determined that the need to increase enrollment and compete successfully with other Catholic, accredited colleges in the area was the initial impetus for adopting standards. Requirements for Latin and Greek and the non-accredited undergraduate degree made these Jesuit institutions unattractive to the growing Catholic population in 1920.

Once the institutions modernized the curriculum and became accredited, they continued to face challenges as new accrediting requirements appeared. Between 1920 and 1935, they were influenced to revise their undergraduate curriculum, raise faculty standards, improve graduate programs, increase their endowments, offer doctoral programs and, after much consideration, to adopt a research orientation for Jesuit American universities.

Most Catholic colleges and universities faced these same issues, although their response depended in part on the orientation of the founding religious community and its goals for the institution. The Catholic University of America was a founding member of the Association of American Universities (AAU) in 1900, and the University of Notre Dame affiliated with the NCA in 1913. The Association of Catholic Colleges established guidelines for its members in 1915 that were similar to those expected by the accrediting agencies. Some adapted more quickly than others (Goodchild, 1986).

The rapid growth of the Catholic elementary and secondary school system by mid-century emphasized the need for educated women religious to teach. Standardization was occurring at all levels as state and district boards of education raised requirements and expectations for teacher certification. Although Catholic school teachers could teach without certification, the development of a strong, credible school system was a significant impetus to improve teacher preparation. Further, as a practical matter, most of the young women entering religious communities were not college educated and did not have teaching experience. In response, some religious communities opened colleges as normal schools for **teaching-sisters** only. Encouraged by successful Catholic women's colleges such as Trinity College in Washington, D.C., the College of Notre Dame of Maryland in Baltimore, St. Mary's College in Notre Dame, Indiana, and Manhattanville College in New York, many of the normal schools developed into women's colleges. In 1941, Sister Madeleva Wolff established the first graduate school of theology for women in the United States at St. Mary's. The College of St. Catherine (now St. Catherine University) was fully recognized by the NCA in 1917 and, in 1937, became the first Catholic college in the United States to have a chapter of Phi Beta Kappa. Although some were small and struggled for resources, these institutions

Teaching-sisters

Catholic women religious who taught in Catholic schools

offered Catholic women, often the children of immigrants, the opportunity to earn an education and enter careers such as teaching and nursing (Stewart, 1994, pp. 379–383). As these colleges matured, many transformed into coeducational institutions and continued their commitment to the disadvantaged. In the 1980s, they became leaders in "ensuring access to higher education for the children of America's second great wave of immigration" (Kennelly, 2002, p. 119).

State and research universities continued to grow in size and number throughout the 20th century. Their commitment to the discovery of new knowledge and in applying that knowledge to real problems increased their popularity and importance. The notion that a university, particularly one supported by the state, should have a strong service orientation was especially prominent in the Midwest and West and the University of Wisconsin provided an exceptional model. In the 1870s, the president of the University of Wisconsin, John Bascom, urged his students to share their expertise broadly and in the following decades the university began summer institutes for farmers and helped develop the dairy industry. In Wisconsin, the concept came to be known as the **Wisconsin Idea** and held that "informed intelligence when applied to the problems of modern society could make democracy work more effectively" (Rudolph, 1962, p. 363). The idea is often credited to University of Wisconsin president Charles Van Hise (a student of Bascom's) who said in a 1904 speech, "I shall never be content until the beneficent influence of the University reaches every home in the state" (University of Wisconsin-Madison, n.d., para. 2). Wisconsin pioneered extension courses, offering a variety of classes and lectures throughout the state. University experts in various fields began to appear and to consult with government agencies on just about everything imaginable, including social issues, economics, and administration.

Wisconsin Idea

knowledge from colleges and universities should be used to solve real problems; higher education should be widely available and useful

As accreditation grew and requirements for faculty increased, institutions that offered doctorates expanded. The need for qualified faculty in every field was felt at institutions of all types throughout the country, and the universities positioned themselves to meet the demand.

Junior and Community Colleges:
Vocational Education

As established colleges and universities continued to evolve during the 20th century, a new type of institution emerged and grew along with them. In 1901, there were eight junior colleges in the United States, all of which were private and each of which enrolled less than 100 students. By 1960, over 800,000 students were enrolled in 663 junior or community colleges (Reynolds, 1965, pp. 8–10). Community and junior colleges developed and grew in several directions simultaneously. As scholars Stephen Brint and Jerome Karabel (1989) have observed, they "catered to different publics, were controlled by different types of authorities, and responded to different social and economic agendas" (pp. 30–31). Brint and Karabel (1989) credit the formation of these institutions to several factors including the support of influential individuals at major universities, local pride, religious enthusiasm, the need for preparatory study in the liberal arts, and interest in vocational training.

Influential university administrators, including William Watts Folwell at the University of Minnesota, Henry Tappan at the University of Michigan, and William Rainey Harper at the University of Chicago supported the idea that the work of the freshmen and sophomore years was secondary in nature and could be turned over to the secondary schools, leaving the work of the university to begin in the junior year (Medsker, 1960). University presidents were interested in creating universities as training and research institutes for the intellectual elite, not in the creation of junior colleges as a means to democratize higher education. The extension of secondary school into a junior college could protect their institutions from an onrush of mediocre students. William Rainey Harper, at Chicago, was the first to put a model into place. In 1892, he separated instruction at the University of Chicago into two divisions: one for the first two years of work and one for the second two years. By 1896, the two divisions were known as the junior college and the senior college. In 1900, he convinced the trustees to give an associate's degree to students who completed work at the junior college, hoping that many would terminate their education at that point and only the gifted would continue to the senior college and graduate work (Brint & Karabel, 1989, pp. 23–25).

The organizational form of the public junior college can be credited to Harper's efforts to persuade Chicago-area high schools to offer college-level courses. Harper convinced J. Stanley Brown, principal of Joliet High School, to expand the high school's curriculum to include college-level courses with the promise that graduates of Brown's school would receive advanced standing at the University of Chicago. So in 1901, Joliet Junior College opened as the country's first independent public junior college. Following Harper's lead, university administrators in other states worked to develop junior colleges that might allow the university to drop the first two years of instruction and concentrate on research and scholarship (Brint & Karabel, 1989, pp. 25–27).

The development of junior colleges was also encouraged by local or community spirit as a means to provide social and economic mobility for the children of farmers, shopkeepers, and other workers. Religious enthusiasm accounted for the founding of a number of private junior colleges, many of which were denominational and sometimes created out of a failing four-year college (Brint & Karabel, 1989). About 75% of junior colleges in 1915 were privately controlled but, whether public or private, religious in nature or not, enrollment continued to grow. By 1922, there were 207 junior colleges enrolling about 16,000 students. Of these 207 institutions, 70 were public and 137 were private (Walters cited in Palinchak, 1973, p. 27).

While not the goal of the early university supporters, by 1918, many of the junior college presidents felt that one major role of the two-year institutions was to bring higher education to the masses. Most no longer had a religious affiliation (two out of three were not religiously based), and the vast majority (both public and private) were liberal arts institutions that emphasized curricula which could be transferred to a senior college (Brint & Karabel, 1989, p. 31). The diversity of these institutions made standardization difficult. In fact, in 1924, Leonard V. Koos published a study describing twenty-one separate purposes of the junior college including education for terminal students, leadership training, occupational training, and to make the real functioning of the university possible (Koos cited in Reynolds, 1965, pp. 12–13).

The lack of shared purpose and direction was one of a number of similar problems junior colleges faced during the first twenty years of their existence. They had some difficulty aligning their courses to meet university requirements and creating policies and procedures to maximize the transferability of their courses yet still meet the needs of their terminal students. In an effort to seek common solutions, the American Association of Junior Colleges (AAJC) was created in 1920. It provided a much-needed forum for the debate about the role and organization of the junior college (Brint & Karabel, 1989, pp. 32–33).

It was the leaders of the AAJC who moved the institutions toward occupational training. Two of those leaders, Leonard Koos and Walter Eells, were professors of education who understood the junior colleges from a university perspective. Koos argued that junior colleges could guide less capable students toward their place in society and Eells believed that it would be unfortunate if all junior college students attempted to enroll in a university and prepare for professions that were not aligned with their talents and abilities. Eells and Koos promoted the idea of terminal vocational education by identifying the potential markets open to community colleges and encouraging the use of intelligence testing and guidance counseling to channel students into the right occupational programs (Brint & Karabel, 1989, pp. 34–38). One major problem they faced was that students did not want terminal vocational education. While the leaders of the vocational movement felt that about 75% of the students in junior colleges should be in terminal vocational programs, the reality in 1938–1939 was that barely one-third of the students were actually enrolled in such programs (p. 62). The students wanted to complete the first two years of university study and continue on, as this was understood to be the surest route to social and economic success (p. 43).

The American Association of Junior Colleges responded to the slow development of vocational programs by forming a committee to investigate terminal (vocational) education. In 1939, the AAJC created the Commission on Junior College Terminal Education which held workshops and conferences in addition to publishing information on the topic. Although much had been done, the leaders of the movement believed there was much progress left to make. In 1940, about 70% of the two-year colleges offered some type of terminal education. About one-third of the terminal students studied business (Cohen & Brawer, 2008,

pp. 247–248). Although some educators still argued that liberal education was the foundation of all true education, the vocational role of the junior colleges received increasing support. Continuing to offer both options, student enrollment rose significantly. In 1938–39, enrollment at junior colleges exceeded 330,000 students (Reynolds, 1965, p. 9). Clearly, a need had been met and realized, although the role of these institutions continued to be debated and most students attended for the college transfer options, not the vocational programs. After World War II, junior colleges and **proprietary schools** provided an educational alternative for veterans who, for a variety of reasons, decided against enrollment at a traditional four-year college. Proprietary schools, which operated to make a profit, grew significantly resulting in the establishment of more than 5,000 schools in the five years following the war (Cohen, 1998, p. 194).

Proprietary schools
schools that operate on a for-profit basis

Standardization

Accreditation and Professional Associations

Institutional diversity is clearly one of the great strengths of the American system. However, as diverse colleges and universities developed without central oversight, they eventually faced questions regarding the equity of admission standards (particularly in relation to high school curriculums in different parts of the country), the transferability of courses, the academic integrity of programs, and the comparative consistency of the degrees they awarded. The national interest in business efficiency was applied to higher education and while individual institutions might be efficient, the system of higher education certainly was not. There were no agreed upon entrance or graduation requirements and no common understanding of a unit of academic credit. Terms such as *college, school, graduate, professional program,* and *major* were not uniformly used or defined across campuses. Entrance requirements were particularly challenging to identify and maintain given the variations in secondary school preparation. Under the leadership of the University of Michigan in the 1870s, the state universities of the Midwest adopted **accreditation** systems whereby schools were certified as doing solid preparatory work or where their exams were an acceptable basis for admission. By the turn of the century, at least

Accreditation
process through which an institution demonstrates that it meets established standards

42 state institutions and 150 others had adopted admission by certificate or some form of accrediting. The college preparatory departments, commonly available in colleges due to inconsistent or nonexistent high school standards, began to disappear (Rudolph, 1977, p. 161). Beginning in New England in 1885, six regional *voluntary associations* of colleges and schools developed that were dedicated to standardizing entrance requirements and better articulating secondary and college academic expectations. Those associations eventually accepted an accrediting mission and some have since changed their names or split into separate commissions for the accreditation of different levels of education. The regional accrediting associations are:

1. Middle States Association of Colleges and Schools: Delaware, the District of Columbia, Maryland, New Jersey, New York, Pennsylvania, Puerto Rico, the U.S. Virgin Islands, and several international locations
2. New England Association of Schools and Colleges: Connecticut, Maine, Massachusetts, New Hampshire, Rhode Island, and Vermont
3. North Central Association of Colleges and Schools: Arizona, Arkansas, Colorado, Illinois, Indiana, Iowa, Kansas, Michigan, Minnesota, Missouri, Nebraska, New Mexico, North Dakota, Ohio, Oklahoma, South Dakota, West Virginia, Wisconsin, and Wyoming
4. Northwest Association of Secondary and Higher Schools: Alaska, Idaho, Montana, Nevada, Oregon, Utah, and Washington; originally also included California and Hawaii
5. Southern Association of Colleges and Schools: Alabama, Florida, Georgia, Kentucky, Louisiana, Mississippi, North Carolina, South Carolina, Tennessee, Texas, Virginia, and Latin America
6. Western Association of Schools and Colleges: California, Hawaii, Guam, the Commonwealth of the Northern Marianas, American Samoa, the Federated States of Micronesia, the Republic of the Marshall Islands, and East Asia

During World War I, the American Council on Education established a Committee on College Standards that was composed of representatives of the principal standardizing bodies who were appointed to try to encourage some degree of uniformity in the creation of college standards. The committee was somewhat successful in this

attempt. However, while trying to represent all segments of higher education, the council found itself in a difficult position between those educators who favored accreditation and those who did not (Selden, 1960, pp. 71–72). Until 1916, institutions that agreed to certain standards (credit hour, admission criteria, graduation requirements, etc.) could apply for membership to one of the regional associations and generally they would be accepted. That changed when the NCA (North Central Association of Colleges and Secondary Schools) first developed an actual accrediting program and, in 1913, published its first list of accredited colleges (Pfnister, 1959, p. 52) notwithstanding the fact that there did not yet exist an established understanding of what a college was or should be.

In addition to accrediting organizations, the College Entrance Examination Board formed, as did various associations of similar institutions such as the National Association of State Universities (1896), the Association of Catholic Colleges (1899), the Association of American Universities (1900), the Association of Land-Grant Colleges (1900), and the Association of American Colleges (1914). Realizing they shared common problems, these groups also had to address the issue of standards. As early as 1870, the U.S. Bureau of Education published an annual list of institutions that granted degrees, but that was the limit of its effort to define such institutions. The first and last attempt by the U.S. government to classify institutions of higher education came in 1911. Subsequent to a request from the AAU (Association of American Universities) that it offer a classification of American colleges and universities, the bureau prepared a new type of list. However, the implications of grades of excellence and inferiority proved explosive and "premature partial publication unleashed a storm of protest from injured institutions." President William Howard Taft prohibited official publication of the list and the AAU took up the task by default in 1913 (Rudolph, 1977, pp. 220–221). The association found support for its work from regional and state accrediting agencies and from the boards of philanthropic organizations that were interested in supporting colleges and universities but were having a very difficult time distinguishing between them. Several foundations, including the General Education Board (1903), the Carnegie Foundation for the Advancement of Teaching (1906), the Carnegie

Corporation (1911), and the Rockefeller Foundation (1913), were involved in the effort to standardize higher education and were successful at offering financial incentives to entice institutions to meet higher standards. The Carnegie Foundation proposed a pension to every college professor employed by an eligible institution. The list of eligible professors was whittled down with the elimination of all state institutions, private institutions with a denominational affiliation, and technical institutes that were not of "college grade" (Rudolph, 1977, pp. 220–222). The offer also came with a price. Borrowing some standards from the Regents Board of the State of New York, the foundation decreed that to be recognized as acceptable for the pension program, a college had to

> require fourteen units of high school credit for admission, each unit signifying five recitations a week throughout the year in one subject [the **Carnegie Unit**]...have at least six...professors giving their entire time to college and university work...a course of four full years in liberal arts and sciences...[and] a "productive" endowment of not less than $200,000. (Carnegie Foundation for the Advancement of Teaching, Annual Report 1906, cited in Rudolph, 1977, p. 222)

Carnegie Unit
standard period of study defining an academic course

In 1906, the first Carnegie list included 45 colleges and universities, but by the end of the first year, that number rose to 52. Although this effort was valuable in establishing a definition of a college course of study (as opposed to that of a high school), it must be remembered that strong state universities and private denominational institutions were not included simply on the basis of their governance structure, without regard for their quality or requirements. Therefore, the list cannot be considered to represent all high-quality institutions at that time. However, it did have a significant impact. Some institutions dropped their religious affiliations to be included, others raised their standards. By 1911, 160 southern colleges and universities required a four-year high school course for matriculation, up from just 5 in 1906. The Carnegie Foundation soon realized that even with restrictions, the pension funds would be too large to manage. So, in 1918, the foundation established an endowment for the Teachers Insurance and Annuity Association (TIAA) and thereby created an organization to which institutions and individuals could contribute in preparation for retirement. Some associations, like the Catholic Education Association, adopted the Carnegie

standards even while additional expectations were being set by other organizations. Requirements for libraries and scientific laboratories came from the Association of American Universities; the American Council on Education dictated teaching hours and class size; and the Carnegie Foundation required that department heads have a Ph.D. (Rudolph, 1977, pp. 222–224).

Efforts to develop a definition of a college continued and, in 1919, the American Council on Education offered one that was supported by both the General Education Board and Carnegie Foundation. According to the American Council on Education, a college was a place:

- that required for admission the completion of a four-year secondary course approved by a recognized accrediting agency and correlated to the college course to which the student was admitted;
- that required for graduation the completion of at least 120 semester hours of credit;
- that supported a faculty of at least eight heads of departments for a student body of one hundred;
- where professors were required to have completed at least two years of graduate school and expected to teach no more than sixteen hours a week in classes of no more than thirty students;
- that required an operating income of $50,000 or more, half derived from permanent endowment;
- that had a library of at least 8,000 volumes exclusive of public documents;
- that did not have a preparatory school operated by the college;
- that had a record of achievement in preparing its students for graduate school. (Rudolph, 1977, pp. 225–226)

The accreditation movement continued to gain strength even though some educators believed it had already gone too far. In 1939, the American Council on Education sponsored a conference on accreditation and former president Samuel Capen, now a seasoned university administrator (he was the chancellor of the University of Buffalo in 1922), came back to condemn the accreditation movement in his speech titled, "Seven Devils in Exchange for One." Formerly a strong advocate of accreditation, Capen had changed his opinion. He believed that accreditation had outgrown itself, and that as few as "10 agencies, including

the regional associations, would be able to do all the accrediting that was necessary" (Selden, 1959, p. 23). Capen found fault with the accrediting agencies that existed in 1939 for the following reasons:

- there were too many;
- their activities were too expensive for the institutions;
- they were selfish in compelling a university to expend money on a given unit even though another unit might suffer as a consequence;
- they measured institutions in terms of money and objects rather than the intellectual quality of their products;
- many of their standards were based on assumptions only; for example, the requirement that there be a minimum endowment of $5,000,000 or that department heads must have a doctorate;
- they interfered in matters of no concern to themselves, such as admission requirements, pre-professional courses, and size of classes. (Selden, 1959, p. 23)

A second meeting on accreditation was held by the American Council on Education in 1940. At this meeting, George A. Works, dean of the University of Chicago, said, "Fundamentally I am opposed to the control of an institution of higher learning by an outside agency. Once chartered by a State, I should like to think of every college or university realizing the ideals that should characterize an institution of higher learning entirely on its own." He believed, however, that accreditation must be tolerated as a "necessary evil" and that the accreditation system was preferable to turning the "work of accreditation over to individual States" (Selden, 1959, pp. 23–24). Although the movement continued to expand, there was no consensus of opinion in the higher education community of 1940 regarding the purpose of, or need for, standards imposed by accreditation agencies.

The purpose and need for accreditation or approval by a nationally recognized organization became clear as federal financial assistance to higher education was increasingly tied more closely to accreditation. Since 1917, the federal government had regularly published a list of federally approved institutions but that directory did "not in any sense constitute accrediting by the Office of Education" (Sanders, 1959, pp. 19–20).

The role of accrediting agencies expanded considerably in 1952 when Congress passed the Veteran's Readjustment Assistance Act. The act stipulated that federal assistance to veterans could only be used for educational programs offered by institutions that were accredited by an accrediting agency that was itself recognized by the U.S. Commissioner of Education. Although voluntary accrediting agencies had existed in one form or another since 1885, through this law the Office of Education was required to "recognize" or approve them for the first time. Since the 1952 act, federal aid to education legislation has been tied to recognized accrediting agencies in at least fifteen other major pieces of legislation including: Health Professions Act of 1963; Vocational Education Act of 1963; Civil Rights Act of 1964; Higher Education Act of 1965; Health Professions Act of 1966; and Educational Professions Development Act of 1967 (Trivett, 1976). Accreditation continued to be required through the reauthorization of these laws and the implementation of new laws and regulations affecting access, athletics, and opportunity in higher education.

National Collegiate Athletic Association (NCAA)

The brutality of college football became obvious as it grew increasingly outrageous. Each year, serious, sometimes fatal, injuries attended the season. In 1905, 18 men died and 146 were critically injured as a result of the game. The president of the United States, Theodore Roosevelt, threatened to abolish football by executive order if the colleges did not clean it up themselves. Bringing the power of his office to bear, Roosevelt called several football leaders to the White House on October 9, 1905, and informed them that they must make the game less dangerous or risk its abolition. The first football rules committee organized and met in Philadelphia but, notwithstanding the president's directive, did not make the game safer. Leadership emerged in the person of Henry M. MacCracken, chancellor of New York University. He called a special meeting of all the colleges and universities that fielded football teams. Thirteen eastern institutions agreed to attend and when they met on December 9, 1905, they agreed to reform the game. Voting to reconvene on December 28th, the group issued another set of invitations. Sixty-two schools sent representatives to the second meeting. Captain Palmer E. Pierce of West Point convinced the delegates to create a formal

organization that was called the National Intercollegiate Football Association. Significantly, the word *football* was later eliminated and the new organization was named the Intercollegiate Athletic Association of the United States (IAAUS). Pierce led the group to accept a formal organization to take collective action and to create their own football rules committee. Rather than directly challenge the original rules committee, he invited its members to join and they agreed to "amalgamate" on a temporary basis. Representatives of the two committees met in January 1906 and elected William T. Reid of Harvard as secretary. This was a decisive move since Reid was a member of the old football rules committee, not of IAAUS. Reid clarified the standing rules and the group (officially called the American Intercollegiate Football Rules Committee) agreed that changes could be adopted by majority vote (rather than by unanimous vote as had been the case under the old committee). Changes were rapidly made including the approval of the forward pass, prohibition against kicking loose balls and hurdling, the establishment of a neutral zone between offensive and defensive lines, reduction of playing time from 70 to 60 minutes, and setting a ten-yard requirement for first downs. Perhaps most important, the committee eliminated mass momentum plays by requiring at least six men on the offensive line at all times. The efforts succeeded and football began to regain public favor during the much safer 1906 season. By 1907, membership in the IAAUS reached 49 (Falla, 1981, pp. 13–17).

The IAAUS was designed to be an association that would be controlled by the will of its members rather than a single man, group, or bloc of institutions. The constitution and bylaws were drawn up by the original executive committee in 1905 and were ratified by thirty-five member colleges and universities. Twenty-eight institutions sent delegates to the convention of 1906 where they proceeded to follow those documents and establish the first official Executive Committee, the members of which would manage the daily business of the association. The articles of the constitution imply that the new organization did not intend to limit its influence to football but expected to supervise and regulate college athletics "in order that the college activities...may be maintained on an ethical plane in keeping with the dignity and high purpose of education" (IAAUS Constitution, cited in Falla, 1981, p. 21). Member institu-

tions agreed to "home rule," meaning that each would be responsible for enforcing the rules and regulations of the IAAUS on their own campuses. So, while bylaws relating to amateurship and eligibility were included, the association did not have any power to enforce them, leaving that to the institutions themselves (Falla, 1981, pp. 20–25).

By 1912, there were ninety-seven colleges and universities in the group, but Princeton, Yale, and Annapolis continued to resist. Aspiring to be positioned as a truly national organization as its membership grew, the IAAUS changed its name to the National Collegiate Athletic Association (NCAA) at the convention of 1910 (Falla, 1981, pp. 35–36). The issue of institutional enforcement continued to be problematic. It was evident that many schools ignored the NCAA regulations in favor of winning teams. Prompted by an NCAA request for an independent review, the Carnegie Foundation agreed to evaluate the state of college athletics. "When the report was issued in 1929, the foundation documented the rampant professionalism, commercialization, and exploitation that were corrupting virtually all aspects of intercollegiate athletics" (Lapchick & Slaughter, 1994, p. 8). The report noted two fundamental causes for the "defects" of American college athletics: "commercialism and a negligent attitude toward the educational opportunity for which the college exists" and further explained:

> We have defined commercialism as that condition which exists when the monetary and material return from sport are more highly valued than the returns in play, recreation, and bodily and moral well-being....
>
> It is the undergraduates who have suffered most and will continue to suffer from commercialism and its results. True, the commercial policy has provided medical attention and hospitalization for injured athletes, but far fewer injuries would have resulted from uncommercialized games. It has rendered attendance at contests held on alien fields for the sake of profits, expensive and almost impossible.... Commercialism motivates the recruiting and subsidizing of players, and the commercial attitude has enabled many young men to acquire college educations at the cost of honesty and sincerity. More than any other force, it has tended to distort the values of college life and to increase its emphasis upon the material and the monetary. (Savage, Bentley, McGovern, & Smiley, 1929, pp. 306–307)

Students no longer gained the value of developing the personal attributes traditionally associated with athletics. They were no longer allowed to use independent judgment on the field and had become "puppets pulled by older hands." The lack of intellectual challenge in athletics, as explained in the report, resulted from the fact that the governance of athletics had been "delivered utterly into the hands of older persons, whose decisions are made with little reference to the benefits that the reasoning process involved might confer upon younger minds" (Savage et al., 1929, p. 309).

Although it acknowledged the problems, the NCAA did little to solve them. The situation continued to escalate and, in 1934, the NCAA adopted new codes of behavior to govern recruiting but continued to rely on self-regulation. Finally, in 1941, a new constitution was ratified that called for the expulsion of members who did not abide by the rules. In a further effort to regulate the practice of offering payments to players, the "sanity code" was passed in 1948 which allowed colleges to fund and offer scholarships to players based on financial need. Still, institutions failed to comply. Within a year, the compliance committee charged Boston College, the Citadel, the University of Maryland, the University of Virginia, Villanova University, Virginia Military Institute, and Virginia Polytechnic University with violations. The committee estimated that as many as twenty other institutions were equally guilty. A motion to suspend membership for the seven institutions that were formally charged failed to receive the required two-thirds vote. Two years later, the sanity code was repealed and institutions were allowed to offer financial assistance to individuals on the basis of athletic ability without regard to financial need (Lapchick & Slaughter, 1994, pp. 8–10).

In the late 1940s and early 1950s, separate scandals involving point shaving, gambling, and illegal recruiting affected more than thirty players in New York State, three at the University of Kentucky, and three more at Bradley University. For the first time, the NCAA placed institutions on probation and went so far as to cancel basketball at the University of Kentucky for a year. That decision cost the University of Kentucky an estimated $150,000 in lost revenue. Bradley University was also placed on probation for the scandal and other violations, including under-the-table payments to team members. The loss of respect combined

with the financial impact sent a clear message, and the NCAA had successfully positioned itself as the "power behind college sport and the defender of ethical behavior" (Lapchick & Slaughter, 1994, p. 10).

Purpose and Policy: Federal Impact

The Constitution of the United States does not empower the federal government with responsibility for education. Consequently, state and local governments have the authority and the obligation to develop and maintain educational opportunities for their residents. The Constitution, however, does not prohibit the federal government from offering financial support for initiatives viewed as important to the national interest. Funding to develop land-grant colleges was an early example of federal largesse to address national goals. In the 20th century, the federal government offered new types of support that were intended to promote research at certain institutions or to encourage individual students to pursue higher education and, in some cases, to entice them to study a particular discipline.

The first federal student assistance program was conducted by the National Youth Administration from 1935 to 1943. Spending $93 million and assisting about 620,000 students, it was designed as a response to the Great Depression of the 1930s (Brubacher & Rudy, 1976, p. 230). Later, as colleges experienced a drop in enrollment during World War II, many survived only through government subsidies that usually arrived in exchange for specialized military training programs. However, for many institutions, survival in the years immediately following the war ceased to be a concern. As Christopher J. Lucas (2006) correctly observes, "No mind-numbing litany of statistics, however extensive and important, could do justice of itself to the growth of American higher education in the postwar period" (p. 252). Nearly half the income of certain institutions came from the national government by 1945. Research grants and training contracts extended into the postwar period as attention to scientific and technical studies in higher education increased. Around 1950, approximately $150 million was being spent by federal agencies for contract research at universities. By 1960, federal support for research programs in universities and their affiliated research centers exceeded $750 million (Lucas, 2006, p. 253).

More far-reaching was the Servicemen's Readjustment Act of 1944 (known as the G.I. Bill) which provided financial support to millions of veterans after World War II. The bill guaranteed veterans "a year of education for 90 days service, plus one month for each month of active duty, for a maximum of 48 months. Tuition, fees, books, and supplies up to $500 a year would be paid directly to the college or university (at a time when private universities charged about $300 per year tuition and state universities considerably less). Single veterans were to receive a subsistence allowance of $50 a month, married veterans $75 a month" (Kiester, cited in Thelin, 2004, p. 263). Toward the end of 1945, substantial revisions were made to the bill that liberalized the terms of government-sponsored loans for the purchase of homes, farms, or businesses; raised the limit on the guarantee for realty loans from $2,000 to $4,000; and extended repayment periods for up to twenty-five years for a home and forty years for a farm. Congress also made significant changes in the benefits for education and training, eliminating the requirements that a veteran prove his education had been previously "interrupted" by the service and that funds paid for education and training be deducted from future bonuses. A veteran could begin a program of study up to four years after discharge (extended from the original two years) and use the benefit for up to nine years (extended from the original seven). Subsistence allowances were also raised from $50 to $65 per month for unmarried veterans and from $75 to $90 per month for veterans with dependents. Fifty-one percent of G.I.s took advantage of the provision for education and training. Approximately 2.2 million attended a college or university and an additional 5.6 million elected some form of sub-college training, often a short course or certificate program (Olson, 1974, pp. 37, 123, 124; Altschuler & Blumin, 2009, p. 83).

Intended to keep returning veterans out of the labor market while business and factories retooled after the war, few expected the G.I. Bill to have a significant impact on higher education. Supporters anticipated about 8% to 10% of eligible veterans would opt to enroll in college. However, by fall 1945, approximately 85,000 veterans had been accepted for participation. Enrollments surpassed 1 million by 1946 and paid benefits exceeded $5.5 billion ($48 billion in year 2000 dollars). Enrollment at colleges and universities doubled between 1943 and 1946. By 1950, about 16% of

eligible veterans had enrolled in higher education (Thelin, 2004, pp. 262–264). That same year, approximately 94%, or about $2,689,000,000, of federal education funds were spent for veterans' training authorized through the G.I. Bill (Congressional Quarterly Service, 1967, "Federal Role," p. 2). It is difficult to determine how many veterans would have attended college without the bill. However, it is clear that the opportunity had a significant impact, as the ranks of the nation's professionals grew to include an additional "450,000 engineers, 180,000 doctors, dentists, and nurses, 360,000 teachers, 150,000 scientists, 243,000 accountants, 107,000 lawyers, and 36,000 clergymen" (Altschuler & Blumin, 2009, p. 86).

Colleges and universities, for the most part, welcomed the veterans by modifying admission requirements and, with the help of Congress, expanding living space. Campus housing was totally inadequate to accommodate the number and needs of veterans, especially those who were married. In 1945, Congress amended the Lanham Act of 1940, which, in its original form, authorized the federal government to construct public housing in connection with the war effort. The amendments allowed the National Housing Administration to rent or build temporary housing units and colleges could apply to have these units moved to their campuses. By August 1946, the Federal Public Housing Administration reported that 101,463 units had been allocated to the nation's colleges, including over 51,700 family dwellings and over 49,700 dormitory-style units. That same year, the American Council of Education reported serious shortages of college classrooms, administration buildings, libraries, cafeterias, and other buildings. Amending the Lanham Act again, Congress authorized the use of surplus war buildings for educational purposes. More than 700 colleges benefited as the Federal Works Agency transferred 5,920 used, temporary structures that provided 18,375,196 square feet of floor space. Even so, the United States Office of Education estimated that this only provided about 78% of the space the colleges urgently needed. In addition to structures, the government allowed colleges to obtain at less than cost over $114 million worth of surplus equipment including classroom furniture, lockers, medical supplies, books, vehicles, and electronics equipment (Olson, 1974, pp. 66–68).

Report of the President's Commission on Higher Education, 1947

The movement toward access and choice in American higher education found many supporters after World War II, but few had a national platform from which to make their case. Dr. George Zook, president of the American Council on Education, was one of those few. In 1947, he suggested to President Harry Truman that a committee be commissioned to examine the current and potential role of higher education in the United States. The President's Commission on Higher Education was created and charged with:

> defining the responsibilities of colleges and universities in American democracy and in international affairs—and, more specifically, with reexamining the objectives, methods, and facilities of higher education in the United States in light of the social role it has to play. (President's Commission, 1947, p. 1)

Zook and the members selected for the commission supported many forms of higher education and access for as many people as might possibly benefit from it. The report, *Higher Education for American Democracy*, noted that as the national economy became more industrialized and more complex, as production increased and national resources multiplied, the American people realized the need for higher education for their children. World War II had caused a fall off in enrollment but after the war, with the aid of the Servicemen's Readjustment Act, enrollment began to grow and, according to the report, "the increase in numbers is far beyond the capacity of higher education in teachers, in buildings, and in equipment" (President's Commission, 1947, p. 1). Recognizing the deficit, the committee noted that military records demonstrated the potential for more veterans to opt into higher education than had already done so. In fact, according to the commission's statistics, the enrollment of 1947–48 could actually double in ten to fifteen years if all eligible veterans decided to enroll and if sufficient facilities and financial means were available. The commission identified a set of events and attitudes that had contributed to the increased need for higher education:

1. Science and invention had diversified natural resources and multiplied new production techniques. This required employees with new skills and greater matu-

rity, while complex technology made broad understanding of social problems and processes essential.

2. The people of America were drawn from the peoples of the world, creating an American nation with an "indefinite number of diverse groups of varying size. Of and among these diversities our free society seeks to create a dynamic unity...we undertake to effect democratic reconciliation, so as to make the national life one continuous process of interpersonal, intervocational and intercultural cooperation."

3. World War II caused a fundamental shift in American foreign policy. The nation's isolationism had been replaced by a new sense of responsibility in world affairs.

4. The coming of the Atomic Age brought opportunities for "tremendous good or tremendous evil," underscoring "the need for education and research for the self-protection of our democracy, for demonstrating the merits of our way of life to other peoples." (President's Commission, 1947, p. 2)

The report noted that the "law of the land" provides equal justice and equal rights for all regardless of race, sex, faith, occupation, or economic status, and that education was necessary to "give effect to the equality prescribed by law" (President's Commission, 1947, p. 5). In addition to guaranteeing equal opportunity and equal rights, "effective democratic education will deal directly with current problems.... Its role in a democratic society is that of critic and leader as well as servant.... Perhaps its most important role is to serve as an instrument of social transition, and its responsibilities are defined in terms of the kind of civilization society hopes to build" (President's Commission, 1947, p. 6). In order to realize this vision, the commissioners encouraged the colleges along with local communities, the states, the educational foundations and associations, and the federal government to agree on certain common objectives and to work together. The commission suggested three principal goals for higher education:

1. Education for the fuller realization of democracy in every phase of living;

2. Education directly and explicitly for international understanding and cooperation;

3. Education for the application of creative imagination and trained intelligence to the solution of social prob-

lems and to the administration of public affairs. (President's Commission, 1947, p. 8)

While the commissioners agreed that good will, tolerance, and the cooperative spirit are necessary for society to function, the report called for social science and social engineering to solve the problems of human relations. Belief in science generally was now transposed into a belief that social science could solve social problems. The report called for an understanding of "self," noting that man's ability to subdue nature had raced ahead of his ability to understand himself or to reconstruct his institutions. "It is imperative that we find not only the will but the ways and means to reorder our lives and our institutions so as to make science and technology contribute to man's well-being rather than to his destruction.... We must bring our social skills quickly abreast of our skills in natural science" (President's Commission, 1947, p. 21).

The commissioners examined the expansion of the American educational system. In 1900, about 700,000 individuals (11% of the 14- to 17-year-olds) were enrolled in the nation's high schools; by 1940, this number had reached 7 million (73% of the age group). College enrollment had also experienced a significant increase. In 1900, fewer than 250,000 were enrolled (about 4% of the 18- to 21-year-olds); in 1940, there were 1.5 million (a little less than 16% of the age group). By 1947, there were 2.35 million, of whom about 1 million were veterans. Although commendable, the commissioners believed enrollment was "substantially below what is necessary either for effective individual living or for the welfare of our society" (President's Commission, 1947, p. 25). According to the U.S. Census Bureau in 1947, there were almost 17 million men and women over 19 years of age who had stopped their schooling at or below the sixth grade. Of these 17 million, 9 million had never attended school or had stopped before completing the fifth grade. In 1947, about 1.6 million (19%) high school age children (14- to 17-year-olds) were not attending any school and over 66% of the 18- and 19-year-olds were not in school or college. The commission believed these facts were "indefensible in a society so richly endowed with material resources" and noted that "we cannot allow so many of our people to remain so ill equipped either as human beings or as citizens of a democracy" (President's Commission, 1947, p. 27). This failure to pro-

vide a reasonable equality of educational opportunity to the youth of the country was a grave charge in the minds of the commissioners. The report noted that for the great majority of American boys and girls, "the kind and amount of education they may hope to attain depends not on their abilities, but on the family or community into which they happen to be born or, worse still, on the color of their skin or the religion of their parents" (President's Commission, 1947, p. 27). The commissioners outlined barriers to equal opportunity:

1. Economic barriers: The commissioners dispelled the old notion that "any boy can get a college education" if he has it in him, noting that low family income, the rising costs of education, and the lack of college facilities create an almost impassable barrier to many talented young people. In 1945, half of the children under 18 years of age were growing up in families with cash income of $2,530 or less.

2. Curriculum barriers: The commission noted that in 1947, the orientation of higher education was toward verbal skills and intellectual interests that did not serve young people who had abilities of a different kind, so that they could not receive "education commensurate with their native capacities...because colleges and universities recognized only one kind of educable intelligence." The commissioners believed that many other aptitudes should be cultivated and higher education had a responsibility to provide programs for the development of abilities other than those that required academic aptitude.

3. Racial and religious barriers: The commission noted that the outstanding example in this area was the situation of the Negroes.* The cumulative effect of unequal opportunity was reflected in the fact that in 1940, the schooling of the Negro was significantly below that of Whites at every level from first grade through college. At the college level, the difference was great: in 1940, 11% of the White population had completed at least one year of college and almost 5% had finished four years; for non-Whites (over 95% of whom were Negroes), only 3% had completed at least one year of college and less than 1.5% had completed four years. On the positive side, between 1900 and 1940, the percentage of Negroes 5 to 20 years old

attending school rose from 31% to just over 64%; Negro youth ages 15–20 attending school increased from 17.5% in 1900 to 33.8% in 1940. This was progress but, according to the commissioners, it was far from sufficient. (President's Commission, 1947, pp. 27–36) *Use of the term "Negro" is retained for historical accuracy.

Writing prior to the 1954 U.S. Supreme Court decision in *Brown v. the Board of Education of Topeka, Kansas,* the commissioners railed against school segregation, arguing that although it may not legally mean discrimination, it usually does mean discrimination in fact and in practice. Colleges and universities were also criticized for their quota systems, which limited admission of "Negroes and Jews." The commissioners called this practice un-American and stated that it cannot be "justified on any grounds compatible with democratic principles" (President's Commission, 1947, p. 35). Proclaiming their faith in education as a means of equalizing the conditions of man, they voiced a concern that the system was in grave danger of being an "instrument for creating the very inequalities it was designed to prevent" (President's Commission, 1947, p. 36). The commissioners urged the American people to set as their ultimate goal an educational system "which at no level—high school, college, graduate school, or professional school—will a qualified individual in any part of the country encounter an insuperable economic barrier to the attainment of any kind of education suited to his aptitudes and interests" (President's Commission, 1947, p. 36) and recommended the following steps:

1. Improve high school education for all "normal youth";
2. Make education through grade fourteen available in the same way that high school education was available;
3. Provide financial assistance to competent students in the tenth through fourteenth grades who would not be able to continue their education without such assistance;
4. Reverse the tendency of increasing tuition and other student fees in the senior college beyond the fourteenth year, and in both graduate and professional schools, by lowering tuition costs in publicly controlled colleges and by aiding deserving students through inaugurating a program of scholarships and fellowships;

5. Expand programs of adult education considerably to make more of it the responsibility of our colleges and universities;

6. Make public education equally accessible to all, without regard to race, creed, sex, or national origin. (pp. 36–39)

The President's Commission (1947) projected future enrollment in ideal terms, noting that a minimum of 4.6 million young people should be enrolled in nonprofit educational institutions beyond the twelfth grade in 1960 and, of this number, 2.5 million should be at the junior college level and 1.5 million at the senior college level; 600,000 should be in graduate and professional schools beyond the first degree (p. 39). They argued for general education, stating that colleges were not adequately contributing to the quality of students' lives as adults because the unity of liberal education had been splintered by overspecialization and, as a result, students were ill-prepared, if at all, for "duties as a man, a parent, and a citizen" (p. 48). Further, "a society whose members lack a body of common experience and common knowledge is a society without a fundamental culture" and will tend to disintegrate into a mere collection of individuals (p. 49). The commissioners believed that "the unity must come…from a consistency of aim that will infuse and harmonize all teaching and all campus activities" (p. 49).

National Defense Education Act (NDEA) of 1958

America needed students of high ability, especially in the sciences. In the 1950s, several studies demonstrated that as many as half of the students in the top 20% of their high school graduating class did not enroll in college (Wolfe, cited in Cohen, 1998, p. 200). There arose a concern that the nation was losing academically talented students and, regardless of socioeconomic status, they needed to be identified and encouraged to go on to college. The National Merit Scholarship Program enabled students with limited financial resources to matriculate and, in 1957, more than 96% of nearly 15,000 who received some level of merit program assistance went to college (Harris, cited in Cohen, 1998, p. 201).

The Soviet Union successfully launched a satellite around the Earth that same year. This event, combined with reports from, among others, the Joint Atomic Energy

Commission and the President's Committee on Scientists and Engineers, led to the conclusion that the United States urgently needed more scientists. Passed in 1958, the National Defense Education Act was a response to this apparent national crisis and moved through Congress with relative ease. The $1 billion program, designed to improve teaching in mathematics, sciences, and foreign languages at all levels, represents the largest federal commitment to general education prior to 1965 (Congressional Quarterly Service, 1967, "Federal Role," p. 26). Highlights of the original ten titles are noted here:

Title I: Declaration of purpose, prohibited federal control of education, and defined terms.

Title II: Authorized the U.S. Commissioner of Education to lend $295 million (plus an estimated $145 million for a three-year phase-out period) to college and university student loan funds to enable needy students to continue their education. Superior students intending to teach in elementary or secondary schools and those with ability in science, mathematics, or modern foreign languages were given preference. Up to 50% of the loans could be forgiven (cancelled) for students who later taught in public elementary and secondary schools.

Title III: Provided matching funds to states for public schools and ten-year loans to private schools for the purchase of equipment to teach science, mathematics, and foreign languages or for minor remodeling to accommodate equipment. Seventy-five million dollars a year was authorized for four years, of which 12% was reserved for private school loans.

Title IV: Authorized 5,500 three-year graduate fellowships with a preference given to individuals who were interested in teaching at the college level. They were available only for study at new or expanded graduate study programs. Each fellowship carried a stipend of $2,000 for the first year; $2,200 for the second; $2,400 for the third; and a yearly allowance of $400 per dependent. An additional $2,500 per year was awarded to the school to support the education of each fellow.

Title V: Authorized $15 million a year for each of the four fiscal years for grants to state educational agencies to establish and maintain testing, guidance, and counseling programs in secondary schools; authorized $6,250,000 for fiscal year 1959 and $7,250,000 for the

next three fiscal years for federal contracts with colleges and universities to develop institutes to improve the preparation of school counseling and guidance personnel.

Title VI: Authorized $8 million per year for colleges to establish advanced institutes for modern foreign languages to better prepare practicing public school teachers; funds were also available to assist students who took advanced foreign language training if they planned to go into some form of public service or to teach languages at a college.

Title VII: Authorized funds for federal grants to public or nonprofit groups and individuals to conduct research on modern teaching aids (television, radio, and motion pictures) and publicize the results.

Title VIII: Added a new title to the Vocational Education Act of 1946 authorizing grants to states to train individuals for employment as highly skilled technicians in occupations requiring scientific knowledge.

Title IX: Authorized the establishment of a Science Information Service by the National Science Foundation to disseminate scientific information and develop new programs to make the information available.

Title X: Various provisions related to other provisions of the act, including administration, committees, improvement of statistical services of state education agencies, and allocations to territories and possessions. Also included here was the requirement that loan recipients swear a loyalty oath to the United States and sign an affidavit disclaiming support of, or belief or membership in, any organization that supported the overthrow of the government. (This requirement was removed in 1962.) (Congressional Quarterly Service, 1967, "Federal Role," pp. 8–9)

Faculty and Administration

Academic Freedom

In the early 1800s, the faculty was composed of religious men, often members of the clergy, whose goal was to prepare men to serve God and society through the acquisition of knowledge. That knowledge was based on scripture and was classical in nature. By the end of the century, the faculty was transforming into an academic professor-

Academic ranks

professorial ranks of instructor, assistant professor, associate professor, full professor

Academic freedom

freedom of the professor to investigate and teach/ publish the results of his/her research without interference

Tenure

lifetime appointment granted after period of probationary service

ate with **academic ranks, academic freedom,** and **tenure.** They were increasingly individuals who held an earned doctorate, identified themselves as members of academic disciplines, and embraced the concept that knowledge could be discovered through inquiry. While classical study continued to support the teaching of the liberal arts, the movement toward curricular "usefulness" required faculty who understood agriculture, mechanics, physics, chemistry, biology, and more. Solving the nation's problems and efficiently supporting its expansion required faculty who were willing and prepared to seek solutions where none previously existed. As a result, the academic professorate was changing as rapidly as the institutions it served.

The foundation for intellectual freedom in the United States was grounded in the ideas of the Enlightenment and was supported by the evolution of civil liberties in France and America. It was strengthened in German universities where students were free to learn, and professors could conduct research to discover truth and freely teach and publish their discoveries without fear of losing their position (Brubacher & Rudy, 1976, p. 314). The German concepts of *Lernfreiheit* and *Lehrfreiheit* were admired by many academics who believed if American universities were truly going to be able to address national problems, professors would require some assurance that their findings, publications, and pronouncements would not have a negative impact on their employment. This was a legitimate concern because, as they began to speak out on various issues of the day, some came under fire from institutional benefactors, particularly those who were also college or university board or trustee members. The rights of donors over professors were clearly defended by Alton B. Parker, a Democratic presidential candidate in 1904 and a former judge of the New York Court of Appeals, who noted:

> Therefore, when in opposition to the wishes or without the consent of the supporters of the institution, any of the faculty persists in a course that must tend to impress upon the tender minds of the young under his charge theories deemed to be false by the foundation whose servant he is, or which, if not strictly false to it, are deemed so by a vast majority of the most intelligent minds of the age, it seems to me that he has abused his privilege of expression of opinion to such an extent as to justify the governing board in terminating his engagement. (Parker, cited in Brubacher & Rudy, 1976, p. 314)

The rights of donors were also assumed by many of the businessmen who began to offer substantial financial support to colleges and universities toward the end of the 19th century. Prior to the Civil War, the largest recorded private gift to any college was $50,000, offered to Harvard by Abbott Lawrence. As corporations grew, so did philanthropy. Sometimes contributions were made by individuals to a single institution, such as the $3.5 million from Johns Hopkins to the university that bears his name or the $34 million from John D. Rockefeller to the University of Chicago. Other times gifts were received through a foundation established and funded to support and influence institutions. In 1902, Rockefeller created the General Education Board with assets of $46 million, Andrew Carnegie founded the Carnegie Corporation with $151 million in assets in 1911, and Mrs. Stephen V. Harkness established the Commonwealth Fund in 1918 with assets of $43 million (Hofstadter & Metzger, 1955, pp. 413–414).

New expectations arrived with this new support. Donors expected to have a significant voice, sometimes the deciding voice, in determining the focus and direction of the institutions they supported. While some donors continued to contribute to institutions in response to a specific request, others were using their own resources to create the institution itself. Jonas Gilman Clark determined to establish a university at Worchester, Massachusetts, and hired G. Stanley Hall as its president. Hall often found himself at odds with his benefactor and was forced into a number of decisions with which he disagreed. Relationships could also be based on strong mutual support and respect, as was the case at Cornell University. The president, Andrew D. White, and the benefactor, Ezra Cornell, shared a common vision for the university and worked together to realize it (Hofstadter & Metzger, 1955, p. 416). The trend toward welcoming businessmen (and their wealth) to the board could be clearly observed between 1860 and 1900, when the percentage of board members who were businessmen, bankers, or lawyers increased from 48% to 64% (McGrath, cited in Hofstadter & Metzger, 1955, p. 416). Businessmen were interested in financing higher education, in part, to influence the work of the universities and their faculty. Faculty members, especially in the social sciences of economics and sociology, had begun to study the problems of the economy, the urban centers, and rural America. They began to question the basic organization of the social structure. Richard Hofstadter and Walter P. Metzger (1955) offer an excellent description of the period and the impetus that called some faculty members to action:

> More than anything else, it was the sense that the world was out of joint that gave rise to this new academic worldiness. By long habituation, Americans had become accustomed to social change: to the movement of rootless populations, to an economy permanently in flux. But the changes that came late in the nineteenth century were changes in the rhythm of change, upheavals in social relations, and they challenged settled assumptions. The traditional morality of individualism and the traditional injunction to get rich had produced an undisciplined wealthy elite that thought itself mightier than the laws and threatened democratic institutions. The classical world of small business and the classical law of competition had given birth to gargantuan trusts that were ruining or enveloping their rivals and were rigging the machinery of the market. Worst of all, the appearance of persistent poverty—hunger in the granary of the world, class war in the classless society, despair in the land of opportunity—put all our social shibboleths on trial. (p. 417)

The cases of Richard Ely (University of Wisconsin), Edward Bemis (University of Chicago), and Edward Ross (Stanford University) brought the issue and importance of academic freedom into public view and demonstrated how fragile and unpredictable that freedom was. In 1894, Ely was tried by a regents committee for supporting union activity and, given the conservative nature of the board, he and his supporters expected him to be fired. Contrary to their fears, however, he was exonerated and the board issued a strong statement in support of academic freedom. Professor Bemis was not as fortunate. He had delivered a speech against the railroad companies while the Pullman strike was in progress. The president of the University of Chicago, William Rainey Harper, was displeased and Bemis was released at the end of the year without a trial (Hofstadter & Metzger, 1955, pp. 425–428). Edward Ross intentionally tested the notion of academic freedom by advocating municipal ownership of utilities, calling for a ban on Oriental immigration, and writing a paper in support of free silver (a Democratic position), all in opposition to the interests and values of Mrs. Leland Sanford—the surviving widow of the university's founder. The pres-

ident, David Starr Jordan, tried to intercede on Ross's behalf and for several years was somewhat successful. However, the patroness was adamant that Ross be released and Jordan conceded on the grounds that the security of the university was more important than any individual. Ross was forced to resign in 1900 (pp. 436–439). A number of complex factors attended these outcomes, but it was obvious to all that academic freedom was a valued concept rather than an inviolate right.

In 1913, a joint committee of the American Economic Association, the American Sociological Association, and the American Political Science Association met in an attempt to generate a set of principles regarding academic freedom and tenure but, due to the complexity of the issues, could only produce a preliminary report. Highly regarded faculty from leading universities took up the cause in earnest and, in 1915, the American Association of University Professors (AAUP) was established (Hofstadter & Metzger, 1955, pp. 474–477). Although the AAUP was not universally accepted by either the public or the professors it intended to protect, it proceeded to publish the *General Declaration of Principles* in 1915, which outlined the importance of academic freedom to a free nation and argued for academic tenure. Examining "(1) the scope and basis of the power exercised by those bodies having ultimate legal authority in academic affairs; (2) the nature of the academic calling; and (3) the function of the academic institution or university," the authors held that the purposes of a university are "(a) to promote inquiry and advance the sum of human knowledge; (b) to provide general instruction to the students; and (c) to develop experts for various branches of the public service" (American Association of University Professors, 1915, paras. 9, 20). In order to fulfill those purposes effectively, the declaration argued for faculty representation on evaluation panels, tenure, and a fair system of due process in cases where dismissal is sought.

The AAUP and the Association of American Colleges came together in 1940 and issued the 1940 Statement of Principles on Academic Freedom and Tenure. Laying out a set of guidelines and a thoughtful rationale for academic freedom and tenure, the authors argued that the "common good depends upon the free search for truth and its free exposition" and that

academic freedom is essential to these purposes and applies to both teaching and research. Freedom in research is fundamental to the advancement of truth. Academic freedom in its teaching aspect is fundamental for the protection of the rights of the teacher in teaching and of the student to freedom in learning. It carries with it duties correlative with rights.

Tenure is a means to certain ends; specifically: (1) freedom of teaching and research and of extramural activities, and (2) a sufficient degree of economic security to make the profession attractive to men and women of ability. Freedom and economic security, hence, tenure, are indispensible to the success of an institution in fulfilling its obligations to its students and society. (American Association of University Professors, 1940, paras. 4–5)

Recognizing that academic freedom carries responsibilities, the authors cautioned that although the professor, as a citizen, should be able to write opinions and speak about them in public, he should be careful to remember that his "special position in the community imposes special obligations" and he must be accurate, respectful of the opinions of others and, when speaking as a citizen, make every effort to indicate that he does not represent the institution (American Association of University Professors, 1940, para. 8).

Between 1915 and 1947, the American Association of University Professors (AAUP) reported seventy-three violations of academic freedom, at least half of which occurred at state universities (Hofstadter & Metzger, 1955, pp. 429–430). Academic freedom was severely tested during the 1950s Cold War era of anti-Communist fever. Senator Joseph McCarthy and the House Un-American Activities Committee led a national effort to identify and prosecute individuals who were thought to be affiliated with, or sympathetic to, communism. Fear that professors might be members of the Communist Party emerged, as they were in positions through which they could both entice students and, depending on their area of expertise, spy on or influence research activities at large universities. Professor George R. Stewart (1950) has documented the "Year of the Oath" in California, which involved a requirement promulgated by the board of regents, that all faculty sign an oath of allegiance that read: "I am not a member of the Communist Party, or under any oath, or a party to any agreement, or under any commitment that is in conflict with my obligations under this oath" (p. 20). Dismissal was

to be the result of non-compliance. Faculty in California objected to the requirement for a number of reasons, including that it established a political test for faculty membership which, many believed, stood in opposition to the state constitution. Further, it assigned guilt by association, without consideration of whether or not an individual had committed any crime and it was being applied selectively, that is, other citizens including state officials were not being required to sign (pp. 22–23). Although, in the end, the California regents rescinded the requirement, Stewart (1950) identifies twelve other cases that represent "the same fundamental problem: that is, the interference of a non-professional board with academic tenure, and…academic freedom" (p. 83) between 1915 and 1944. While not all related to communism, these cases illustrate the challenges faculty faced in the 20th century when their views conflicted with the political, economic, or social policy of influential stakeholders.

In 1970, the AAUP and the Association of American Colleges met to reconsider the 1940 Statement of Principles. The result was the publication of the 1970 Interpretive Comments designed to clarify and supplement points in the original document. It is interesting to note that although the AAUP has no authority over institutions or power to enforce its positions, higher education has generally come to endorse the opinions and guidelines outlined in the 1940 document and the comments of 1970. Many incidents over the years have tested academic freedom and pushed its limitations. Faculty members and administrators continue to turn to these documents for support and direction in matters of faculty rights, responsibilities, and due process.

Administration

The development of an administrative structure and its attendant hierarchy had advanced sufficiently during the latter part of the 19th century so that in 1900, Charles Thwing was able to author the book *College Administration*, which claimed to be the first devoted to the topic. Where once the president and the faculty were primarily responsible for the organization and direction of a small institution, by the turn of the century, governing boards of trustees were commonly composed of businessmen and presidents. They were men of the world rather than clergy. Presidents spent more time in public than in the classroom, if they spent any time there at all, and led a staff that included one or more deans, a registrar, and a bursar along with their assistants and secretaries. Institutional size and diversification contributed to the growth of administration, as did varying educational philosophies, the emergence of academic departments, and the presence of larger numbers of students. Higher education was becoming, at the same time, both "fragmented and centralized" (Veysey, 1965, p. 311). In an earlier period, faculty worried about student conduct and codes to control it, but as the universities grew and faculty became more diverse, expectations for faculty productivity, conduct, and appropriate professional requirements for promotion became a matter of faculty and administrative concern (pp. 302–317). Faculty often tended to align themselves more strongly with their discipline than with the institution. According to Veysey (1965), "the multiplicity of cleavages demanded a general submission to regulation, from top to bottom, if all vestiges of order were not to disappear. Bureaucratic modes served as a low but tolerable common denominator, linking individuals, cliques, and factions who did not think in the same terms" (p. 315). Although the administration originated in response to an organizational need and adopted a role that in previous generations had been the purview of the faculty, over time the faculty found that a structure with agreed upon rules could also protect them

> from autocratic superiors…[and] the bureaucratic apparatus also began serving the professor in a less obvious fashion. It became a buffer which protected the isolation of the individuals and the small factions on each campus. Thus if the maze of officials and committees grew sufficiently complex, the whole machinery might screen the faculty member from the administration. Surrounded by politely affirmative deans and committees, the university president gradually lost touch with what was actually going on in "his" classrooms. This could mean that the professor, as long as he avoided sensationalism, became in practice relatively free of intrusion. One speculates that a large measure of academic freedom came about in just such an unintended way. (Veysey, 1965, p. 317)

Changes in the nature of academic life also affected the student experience. The old colonial college exuded a genuine concern for the student's personal well-being but, over time, that had been lost as faculty developed a stronger disciplinary focus and felt the pressure to conduct

research and publish. As one consequence of this redirection of faculty energy, faculty became less able and less interested in devoting time to the personal problems and issues that students faced. So, while the extracurricular activities in which students were involved were fundamental to the students, those activities were not connected to academic life in meaningful ways. Early in the 20th century, educators began to recognize that this proliferation of the extracurriculum was occurring outside of the academic purpose of the college. They recognized a value in the integration of all aspects of a student's life and sought to offer resources, guidance, career advice, professional expertise, and a residential system to support academic and personal development. Through their efforts, a new class of student personnel administrators appeared whose focus was student life (Brubacher & Rudy, 1976, pp. 330–336). Over the course of the century, as students diversified and enrollment grew, this population of administrators expanded and became responsible for all aspects of student life outside the classroom including admission, financial assistance, orientation, residential life, student conduct, career planning, student activities, and athletics.

The growth of organizational structure in the late 18th and early 19th centuries made the "empire-building" of the 20th century possible even without specific shared institutional values. Thus, while unity of purpose disintegrated, a uniformity of standardized practices was coming into being" (Veysey, 1965, p. 311).

Student Life

Student Life and Demographics

Perhaps the most dramatic change in student life was in the students themselves. Over the course of the 20th century, higher education became widely accessible to new populations. Their entrance changed campus life significantly. In 1900, there were about 237,592 undergraduates who accounted for about 4% of the college age group; 40% were women. An additional 5,668 students were in graduate programs. As insurance against downward social mobility, a degree assured your life would be as good as or better than that of your parents. For traditional White students, college meant "good times, pleasant friendships, and...the expectation of life-long prestige resulting from a degree" (Veysey, 1965, pp. 269–272). As scholar Lynn D. Gordon (1990) points out, "For both sexes, but especially for women, student life during the Progressive Era reflected off-campus political and social reform movements and closely linked collegiate activities to preparation for leadership in those areas" (p. 1).

However, different institutions served different populations, and the experiences of students varied greatly. During the early part of the 20th century, coeducation was not universally accepted and education for Black students was often vocational in nature, directing them into the roles social norms had set. As the century progressed, increasing numbers of colleges admitted both men and women and additional opportunities for a liberal education became available to growing numbers of Black students at historically Black colleges and northern institutions.

The improvement of professional schools, the growth of two-year and junior colleges, the development of research universities, the utility of agricultural and technical programs at the land-grant colleges, and the expansion of graduate programs resulted in a growing higher education system that offered something for almost everyone. When the veterans entered this system in tremendous numbers, the system and the infrastructure expanded to accommodate them. All across the country, enrollment increased throughout the 20th century. By mid-century, institutions of higher education awarded almost 500,000 degrees, up from about 29,000 in the 1899–1900 academic year. The number of students doubled about every fifteen years along with the number of faculty. The number of Ph.D.s doubled about every eleven years (Lucas, 2006, pp. 247–248).

Student organizations grew in size and diversity. Fraternal organizations that began in the previous century had displaced literary societies and continued to gain in popularity. In 1865, there were 25 national fraternities; by the mid-20th century, there were 77 along with an additional 45 national sororities (Brubacher & Rudy, 1976, p. 129). Early in the 20th century, Black Greek-letter organizations also developed, primarily in response to the lack of social opportunities available to Black students at predominately White institutions. The first, Alpha Phi Alpha, was thus organized at Cornell University in 1906; the second, Kappa Alpha Psi, at Indiana University in 1911; and in 1922, the Sigma Gamma Rho sorority was established at Butler

University in Indiana. Greek life also developed at historically Black colleges and universities, including 5 national organizations that were created at Howard University between 1908 and 1920 (Torbenson, 2005, pp. 60–61).

During the first six decades of the 20th century, in response to student interest, new student organizations formed including radio, television, drama, music, and dance clubs; ethnic associations; and groups with a focus on an academic discipline, community service, or international discovery. Athletics, especially football and basketball, continued to gain in popularity and the introduction of radio and, later, television brought the games to the audience and increased the pressure to win.

Standardized Testing

By mid-century, federal financial aid made enrollment possible for thousands of individuals who might not have considered it otherwise. The availability of funding and the opportunity to increase enrollment prompted institutions to compete for students, expand housing, and enhance support services. New programs in engineering, science, and other technical fields made higher education more relevant to individuals with diverse aptitudes and career aspirations. Opportunities for rewarding employment in these fields were on the rise. Institutions were interested in identifying potential students who could succeed in them but administrators had no mechanism to judge potential talent on a national scale.

The College Entrance Examination Board, founded in 1900, administered the "college board," which consisted of a weeklong set of essay tests in various subjects that, according to Nicholas Lemann (1999), were designed "to perfect the close fit between New England boarding schools and Ivy League colleges" (pp. 28–29). The president of Harvard College, James Bryant Conant, wanted something else. He wanted an admissions test that would identify high-ability public school boys from outside New England. He wanted a test to ensure that the most meritorious individuals were admitted to the best colleges and universities. In the 1940s, Henry Chauncey (formerly an assistant dean at Harvard) became the head of the College Board and later the president of the Educational Testing Service which opened in January 1948. To identify and support a new elite to lead postwar America, the multiple-

choice Scholastic Aptitude Test (SAT) that the organization promoted could be electronically scored which, it was thought, would eliminate personal grading bias (Lemann, 1999).

A competing exam, known as the ACT (named for the organization that administers it: the American College Testing Service), was developed by psychologists at the University of Iowa to combine admissions decisions with area of study and choice of major (Thelin, 2004). These tests have generated an enormous testing industry complete with fees, test schedules, preparation books, and classes designed to raise scores. They have become a requisite admission component at most American colleges and universities. Yet the question remains as to whether such standardized tests truly identify those students with academic aptitude or merely measure achievement. Perhaps more important, debate continues as to whether they serve to open the doors of higher education and opportunity for all or decisively curb opportunity for those whose socioeconomic status and resultant educational preparation are limited.

GLOSSARY

Great Depression: economic collapse that began in October 1929 and lasted about a decade

Comprehensive colleges: Post-secondary institutions that offer bachelor's and master's degree programs

Industrial education: programs designed specifically to prepare an individual for a vocation

Teaching-sisters: Catholic women religious who taught in Catholic schools

Wisconsin Idea: knowledge from colleges and universities should be used to solve real problems; higher education should be widely available and useful

Proprietary schools: schools that operate on a for-profit basis

Accreditation: process through which an institution demonstrates that it meets established standards

Carnegie Unit: standard period of study defining an academic course

Academic ranks: professorial ranks of instructor, assistant professor, associate professor, full professor .

Academic freedom: freedom of the professor to investigate and teach/publish the results of his/her research without interference

Tenure: lifetime appointment granted after period of probationary service

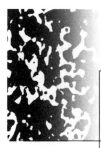

Access and Choice, 1960—the 21st Century

Introduction

The 1960s and 1970s will be long remembered as a period of extraordinary social unrest. Between 1963 and 1968, President John F. Kennedy, Malcolm X, the Reverend Martin Luther King Jr., and Senator Robert F. Kennedy were assassinated. Ten years after the U.S. Supreme Court decided the case of *Brown v. the Board of Education of Topeka, Kansas* and declared that separate was, in fact, not equal, little had changed in many parts of the country. The **Civil Rights Act of 1964**, signed by President Lyndon B. Johnson on July 2nd, outlawed segregation in businesses and banned discrimination in employment and public places, including schools and libraries. Even so, segregation and discrimination continued to limit opportunities for many citizens. In the 1960s, the **Civil Rights Movement** attempted to facilitate change through nonviolent demonstrations in dozens of cities. Campus protests in support of civil rights and against U.S. involvement in the Vietnam War (and the involuntary draft into service that accompanied it) resulted in the development of overt and covert student organizations that pitted themselves against the Federal Bureau of Investigation, regional police, and the

Civil Rights Act of 1964
outlawed segregation in businesses and banned discrimination in employment and public places

Civil Rights Movement
organized effort to secure civil rights, primarily through nonviolent means

National Guard. The resulting violence brought death to campus.

In 1960, the Federal Drug Administration approved the oral contraceptive known as "the pill" effectively separating women's sexuality from fertility. The Feminist Movement, or Women's Liberation, began many years before the 1960s but grew in popularity in the last quarter of the 20th century as women sought full equality in social relationships and public affairs. As greater numbers of women entered the workforce, they fought for equal opportunity and compensation. At the same time, the hippie counterculture, embracing free love, peace, and communal living spread from San Francisco across the country. The mantra "Make Love, Not War" echoed across a small farm in New York State as a half-million young people arrived for the Woodstock Festival and experienced four days of peace and music at the outdoor concert. The generation gap widened.

During this period, the world witnessed the tremendous advances the United States made in science and technology, successfully landing the first humans on the moon in 1969. In the following decades, personal computers revolutionized the way people work, allowing rapid calculation, data manipulation, information storage, and communication. Mobile phones, followed by cell phones, were developed offering convenience and accessibility. A new era of global communication arrived when the World Wide Web was created with the installation of the first Web server outside of Europe in December 1991. In time, online social networks and text messaging would gain in popularity, replacing more traditional forms of communication. By the end of the 20th century, popular attention was concerned with environmental issues, including global warming and an interest in renewable energy. The wars in Afghanistan and Iraq, continued conflict in the Middle East, fear of nuclear proliferation, and political instability in various parts of the world contributed to a general sense of apprehension while a global recession and the collapse of the U.S. housing market in the early 21st century caused tremendous personal economic hardship for many. Barack Obama, the first African American to be elected president of the United States, took office on January 20, 2009, signifying a transformational change that could only have been imagined in the dreams of the 1960s.

Higher Education Access and Choice: Expanding the Federal Role

Elementary and Secondary Education Act, 1965
legislated sweeping education reform aimed at elementary and secondary levels

In 1965, Congress passed the first significant general school aid program. The **Elementary and Secondary Education Act** authorized $1 billion for a variety of programs designed to assist needy children. Although previous administrations had tried, President Johnson (a former teacher) along with a Democratic Congress succeeded in passing sweeping education reform. The legislation was not without critics, and the debate reflected deep and long-standing philosophical differences that had been argued during previous administrations. Proponents favored a broad, strong program of federal aid to public elementary and secondary schools based on the belief that the level of quality of American education was a national concern that could no longer be left to the states. They pointed to high levels of illiteracy, especially in poor states; crowded class-rooms caused by the lack of building during the war and the population growth after it; underpaid teachers who were leaving the profession; poorly prepared teachers; and the belief that states did not have the resources to address all of these problems. Opponents believed just as strongly that education was historically and appropriately a state and local responsibility and warned that federal aid would be followed by federal regulations and control. They believed the proponents were exaggerating the problems without demonstrating a legitimate need (Congressional Quarterly Service, 1967, "Federal Role," pp. 3–5). Questions concerning the appropriate federal role and the level of support were debated along with questions of principle:

- Could federal aid to districts maintaining racially seg-regated schools in open defiance of the law of the land be justified on the grounds that only with Southern votes could a bill be passed?

- At what point would federal aid to private schools exceed constitutional boundaries or denial of such aid become discriminatory? Would the principle of separa-tion between church and state be jeopardized?

- What should be the shape and scope of federal aid? Would aid to teachers' salaries enhance the possibility of federal control; or would a construction-only pro-gram itself be a form of control? (Congressional Quarterly Service, 1967, "Federal Role," pp. 3–4)

Early versions of the Elementary and Secondary Education Act aided only the poorest states. Later, wealthier states were included based partly on the belief that a national foundation of funds should be established to augment state resources. In the end,

> the Elementary-Secondary Act funds would reach an estimated 95% of the counties in the United States. Further, the 1965 Act contained very few restrictions on the dispersal of funds, leaving this mainly to the state education agencies. The local districts could spend the funds in any way approved by these agencies (with final approval by the U. S. Office of Education), provided they took into account the needs of poor children who attended non-public schools. (Congressional Quarterly Service, 1967, "Federal Role," p. 5)

Passage of this bill was a tremendous success for the Johnson administration. Still, the administration's "war on poverty" required a multifaceted approach and funding for lower levels of education was followed by the passage of the Higher Education Act of 1965 which provided unprecedented support for higher education.

The Higher Education Act of 1965

Higher Education Act of 1965
focused on improving postsecondary education and provided significant financial aid for students

The **Higher Education Act of 1965** brought sweeping change to postsecondary education. Authorizing $804,350,000 in fiscal year 1966 and containing eight titles (most of which were funded for three years) the act established important new programs to aid students and colleges. With passage of this legislation, the federal government assumed significant responsibility for ensuring access to higher education for individuals from disadvantaged socioeconomic groups. Highlights of the original eight titles include:

Title I: Community Service and Continuing Education: Authorized federal matching funds to the states for the development of community service programs with a focus on urban and suburban problems such as housing, transportation, and health. The programs were to be administered by public or private nonprofit colleges or universities.

Title II: College Library Assistance and Training and Research: Authorized $50 million annually in fiscal years 1966–68 in grant funds to assist institutions of higher education to improve library resources; also

funded training of librarians and information science specialists and provided resources for the Library of Congress to improve its cataloguing service and acquire additional materials.

Title III: Strengthening Developing Institutions: Authorized, in fiscal year 1966, $55 million to improve the academic quality of "developing" institutions defined as colleges that are struggling to survive and are "isolated from the main currents of academic life." Of this appropriation, 78% was allocated to institutions that award the bachelor of arts degree and 22% to two-year institutions.

Title IV: Student Assistance: Authorized federally funded educational opportunity grants and federally insured student loans with interest subsidies for full-time students. The work-study programs authorized under the 1964 Economic Opportunity Act were transferred here, and the bill also amended several sections of the 1958 National Defense Education Act. Among other items, Part A authorized $70 million annually in fiscal years 1966–68 for grants to institutions for first-year, full-time students who showed exceptional financial need. Funding necessary to continue beyond the first year was also assured. Institutions were required to review each applicant's financial need and to establish programs to encourage academically able but financially needy students to attend college. Part B authorized the U.S. Commissioner of Education to strengthen student loan insurance programs and pay interest subsidies for students of families whose adjusted gross income was $15,000 or less; to establish requirements for institutional participation and student repayment; and to set limits on interest rates and student borrowing. Part C transferred authority for the work-study program to the Office of Education and made several revisions to the previous legislation. Part D amended Title II of the National Defense Education Act in terms of student loan repayment requirements and forgiveness policies.

Title V: Teacher Programs: Directed the U.S. Commissioner of Education to establish an Advisory Council on Quality Teacher Preparation to examine the effectiveness of the title's programs in recruiting, preparing, and retaining teachers for elementary and secondary schools. Part B established a National Teachers

Corps in the Office of Education. Recognizing the need to improve the quality of elementary and secondary education, Part C authorized the development of fellowships for graduate study for teachers and others in related educational fields such as librarians, social workers, and guidance counselors.

Title VI: Improvement of Undergraduate Courses: Provided matching federal grants to institutions of higher education to improve classroom instruction. For fiscal year 1966, $35 million was allocated for laboratory and audiovisual equipment; printed material (other than textbooks); courses in science, the humanities, arts, and education; and minor remodeling. Fifty million dollars was allocated for fiscal year 1967 and $60 million for fiscal year 1968. Additional funds were made available for closed-circuit television equipment and additional forms of minor remodeling.

Title VII: Amendments to the Higher Education Facilities Act of 1963: Increased the grant for undergraduate facilities to a total of $460 million (a $230 million increase for fiscal year 1966); increased the allocation for graduate facilities to a total of $120 million (a $60 million increase for fiscal year 1966); and revised some of the requirements for use of the money.

Title VIII: General Provisions: Defined "higher education" to include nonprofit two- and four-year colleges, technical institutions, and business schools; and it included under the term "state," the District of Columbia, Puerto Rico, Guam, American Samoa, and the Virgin Islands. This section also made it clear that nothing in this legislation authorized federal control over administration, curriculum, personnel, or library holdings and noted that aid to any school (or department) of divinity, or any educational activity that was sectarian or religious in nature, was prohibited. (Congressional Quarterly Service, 1967, "Federal Role," pp. 50–54)

As a result of the Higher Education Act of 1965, the commissioner of education was required to compile a list of all institutions eligible to participate in the extensive student financial assistance programs that the act created. In order to manage this, in 1968, the commissioner established the Accreditation and Institutional Eligibility Staff (AIES) with an advisory committee. The purpose of the

AIES was to administer criteria and procedures for approving accrediting agencies, list them, and determine preliminary eligibility of institutions (Trivett, 1976). Federal influence over accreditation expanded with the reauthorization of the Higher Education Act in 1992. The bill identified areas that accreditors must include in both their standards and reviews, "including curriculum, faculty, and student achievement...and established the National Advisory Committee for Institutional Quality and Integrity (NACIQI) as the group making recommendations to the secretary of education regarding the recognition of accrediting agencies" (Brittingham, 2009, p. 23).

Accreditation remains a voluntary activity controlled by professional associations although all federal funding and most foundation funding require that eligible institutions be accredited. So, while not directly responsible for accreditation, private foundations and the federal government have successfully used their spending power to influence the direction of higher education in the United States. The impact of federal financial aid is readily apparent. Sixty-two percent of all undergraduates and 74% of all graduate students received some form of financial aid in 2007–08. The average received was $9,100 and $17,600, respectively (Wei, Berkner, He, Lew, Cominole, & Siegel, 2009, p. 3).

State governments were, and continue to be, the single largest source of financial support for higher education, but the Higher Education Act established a significant role for the federal government. Regularly reauthorized since 1965, the law has expanded federal financial assistance to students and supported the development and improvement of numerous institutions. Periodic reauthorization has also resulted in the addition of new expectations that have expanded or changed the student experience. For example, in 1972, the Education Amendments included Title IX which requires gender equity for males and females in any education program or activity that receives federal funds (Title IX, Education Amendments of 1972, Section 1681). Amended by the Civil Rights Restoration Act of 1987, "program or activity" was expanded to require broad, institution-wide application of Title IX to "all of the operations" of a wide range of organizations, corporations, and educational institutions (Civil Rights Restoration Act, 1987, Sections 2- 3). In higher education, the law forbids dis-

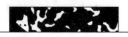

crimination based on gender at all post-secondary institutions that receive any federal financial assistance and applies to all institutional services, including but not limited to academic programs, admission, financial aid, housing, athletics, grading, and student activities. The law has had a significant impact, especially in the area of athletics, where the requirement for gender equity has resulted in the development of new opportunities for women to participate in sports at the collegiate level.

No Child Left Behind Act of 2001

As in the past, access to higher education rests in large part on accessibility to high-quality preparation at the elementary and secondary levels. In many areas of the country, particularly in large urban centers, educational preparation is inconsistent or insufficient. As a result, significant numbers of young people are unable to take advantage of the opportunities available through higher education. The **No Child Left Behind Act (NCLB) of 2001** was the title given to the reauthorized Elementary and Secondary Education Act. Intending to increase accountability and transparency, the NCLB requires national standardized testing at the elementary and secondary levels and established consequences for schools that do not meet their adequate yearly progress targets. A significant amount of data have been gathered although there is not yet a consensus regarding the act's effectiveness in assuring educational quality.

No Child Left Behind Act of 2001 reauthorization of the Elementary and Secondary Education Act intended to increase accountability and transparency

A Test of Leadership: Charting the Future of U.S. Higher Education (2006)

In 1983, the National Commission on Excellence in Education focused public attention on serious deficiencies in the school system with the publication of *A Nation at Risk: The Imperative for Educational Reform* (National Commission, 1983). Over twenty years later, U.S. secretary of education Margaret Spellings established a commission and charged it to "consider how best to improve our system of higher education to ensure that our graduates are well prepared to meet our future workforce needs and are able to participate fully in the changing economy. To accomplish this purpose, the Commission shall consider Federal, state, local, and institutional roles in higher education and analyze whether the current goals of higher education are appropriate and achievable" (U.S. Department of Education, 2006, "A Test," p. 33). The final report, published in September 2006 recognized the tremendous success of postsecondary education but strongly cautioned against complacency and called for "dramatic improvement" (p. ix). The commission noted that "ninety percent of the fastest-growing jobs in the new knowledge-driven economy will require some postsecondary education...the median earnings of a U.S. worker with only a high school diploma are 37% less than those of a worker with a bachelor's degree. Colleges and universities continue to be the major route for new generations of Americans to achieve social mobility. And for the country as a whole, future economic growth will depend on our ability to sustain excellence, innovation, and leadership in higher education" (p. 1). Focusing on six areas, the commissioners identified the following issues and offered relevant recommendations:

Access

Issues: Substandard high school preparation was compounded by poor alignment between high school requirements and the expectations of colleges and employers. While high school graduation rates had increased, the college completion rate failed to improve at the same rate. Further, there remained a persistent gap between the college attendance and graduation rates of low-income students and others of more affluent means. Just 18% of Blacks and 10% of Latinos in the 25–29 age range had obtained a bachelor's degree compared to one-third of their White counterparts.

Recommendations: Higher education needs to work closely with the K–12 system to ensure that "teachers are adequately trained, curricula are aligned, and entrance standards are clear" (p. 17), and incentives are necessary to support long-term commitments to assist underserved students prepare for and remain in college. Students and parents need more information to understand the value of a college degree and realize the academic and financial requirements necessary for success. Appropriate resources including academic support, college planning, and financial aid application assistance are

required early in their academic careers so that these issues do not become barriers.

Cost and Affordability

Issues: Citing the "seemingly inexorable" increase in college costs the commissioners expressed concern that the cost discouraged student attendance or required students to accept significant debt. "From 1995 to 2005, average tuition and fees at private four-year colleges and universities rose 36% after adjusting for inflation. Over the same period, average tuition and fees rose 51% at public four-year institutions and 30% at community colleges" (p. 10). While recognizing the importance of this issue to families, the commissioners also acknowledged its impact on taxpayers who support higher education at both the federal and state levels. Noting that "as institutional costs go up, in recent years state subsidies have decreased on a per capita basis and public concern about affordability may eventually contribute to an erosion of confidence in higher education" (p. 2) the commissioners attributed the problem to a financing system that lacks incentives for colleges and universities to improve efficiency and productivity. Further, they observed that institutions must comply with over 200 federal laws that may waste resources while producing little real benefit.

Recommendations: Higher education should develop new performance benchmarks and reduce barriers for transfer students (lowering the per-student educational cost) to improve institutional cost management. State and federal policymakers should support the spread of technology that can lower costs by relieving the regulatory burden on colleges and universities and encouraging more high school–based college courses (p.2).

Financial Aid

Issues: The commissioners noted that there were a minimum of twenty separate federal programs that offered direct financial aid or tax relief to postsecondary students as part of a financial

aid system which is "confusing, complex, inefficient, and frequently does not direct financial aid to students who truly need it" (p. 3). They expressed concern over the fact that families often do not receive notice of their financial aid awards until spring of the senior year of high school, which makes planning difficult. Further, unmet need was a growing problem, especially for low-income students. Among families with the lowest income (below $34,000 annually) unmet financial need rose by 80% from 1990 to 2004 at four-year institutions (p. 12).

Recommendations: Replace the system of financial aid programs with one that is more in line with student needs and national priorities. This would require restructuring the financial aid system and significantly increasing need-based aid. The commissioners recommended that the Free Application for Federal Student Aid (FAFSA) be replaced with a much simpler form and the whole process be streamlined. Federal grant programs should be consolidated, and the purchasing power of the Pell Grant increased over a five-year period to a level of 70% (from 48% in 2004–05) of the average in-state tuition at a public four-year institution. They advised that colleges and universities develop strategies to contain costs so that this new funding is not simply absorbed into rising tuition (p. 19).

Learning

Issues: The commissioners expressed concern that, based on the evidence, the "quality of student learning at U.S. colleges and universities is inadequate and, in some cases, declining" (p. 3). Employers reported that many recent graduates were not prepared to work and lacked critical thinking, writing, and problem-solving skills. There was an urgent need for workers at all stages to upgrade skills but national, state, and institutional policies and practices often failed to provide the financial and logistical support necessary for lifelong learning. In the view of the commissioners, this problem was exacerbated by transfer systems that did not facili-

tate easy movement between different types of institutions.

Recommendations: The commissioners recommended a series of related steps beginning with stronger accountability systems, outlined under the heading "Transparency and Accountability," and including a commitment by postsecondary institutions to "new pedagogies, curricula, and technologies to improve student learning" (p. 4).

Transparency and Accountability

Issues: The commissioners expressed concern regarding the "remarkable shortage of clear, accessible information about crucial aspects of American colleges and universities" (p. 4). Data systems, they argued, were limited and inadequate making it difficult for policy makers and the public to make informed decisions and preventing higher education from "demonstrating its contribution to the public good" (p. 4).

Recommendations: The commissioners recommended that colleges and universities become more transparent about "cost, price, and student success outcomes" (p. 4) and share this information with students and families. Institutions should measure student success on a "value-added" basis, taking into account students' academic baseline when assessing results. This information should be available to the public in aggregate form, providing an understandable way to measure the relative effectiveness of different institutions of higher education. To this end, the commissioners recommended that the secretary of education require the National Center for Education Statistics to generate public reports of college revenues and expenditures, including an analysis of major changes from year to year, at the sector and state levels. Further, the commissioners supported a student-level data system that would allow policy makers and consumers to evaluate "the performance of institutions by determining the success of each institution's students without knowing the identities of those students" (p. 22).

Innovation

Issues: Barriers to investment in innovation have limited the ability of postsecondary institutions to address workforce needs. Curricula and research funding largely remain within individual departments even though innovation tends to occur at the "intersection of multiple disciplines" (p. 16). Noting that few institutions embraced an entrepreneurial approach, the commissioners also recognized that state and federal policy makers had failed to make innovation a priority. Government regulation and accreditation, they conceded, also hampered the development of new approaches.

Recommendations: The commission urged colleges and universities to "embrace a culture of continuous innovation and quality improvement" (p. 5); develop new pedagogies, curricula, and technologies to improve learning; and to pay particular attention to the areas of science and mathematics. Simultaneously, a national strategy for lifelong learning was needed to support continuous education. (U.S. Department of Education, 2006, "A Test")

Financing Higher Education

During the last quarter of the 20th century, Michael S. McPherson and Morton O. Schapiro (1991) studied funding trends in higher education and recognized that the most important source of revenue in public higher education was appropriations from state and local governments "which provided over 60% of educational and general revenue at these institutions in the 1985–86 academic year" (p. 4). While federal financial aid programs tended to target high-needs students, state and local appropriations generally worked to keep tuition low for all students in support of public higher education. "As a result, student tuition and fees (including all payments from student aid) supplied only 18% of revenue at public institutions in the 1985–86 school year" (McPherson & Schapiro, 1991, p. 4). The most important sources of revenue at private, nonprofit institutions were, and continue to be, tuition and fees which, during this same period, provided about half of the educational and general revenue. Federal support was next in impor-

tance and provided about 22% of revenue although it should be noted that most of the funding supported research and was concentrated in a few select universities (p. 4). McPherson and Shapiro (1991) report that in 1985–86:

> Of the total college and university revenue of $81 billion...
> the federal government contributed about $8.1 billion of
> it through student aid. This compares to payments from
> state and local governments of over $30 billion. The federal
> and state contributions are, of course, distributed quite
> differently among types of institutions. Some 98% of state
> expenditures on higher education are devoted to public
> institutions. The federal expenditures are spread wider,
> with about one-half going to public institutions, one-
> quarter to private, nonprofit institutions, and the final
> quarter, to profit-seeking trade and vocational schools.
> The relatively large percentage of support going to pro-
> prietary institutions, relative to their enrollments (which
> are between 5% and 7% of the total), reflects the fact that
> their student bodies are disproportionately drawn from
> lower income groups and the fact that their tuition charges
> are high enough to qualify their students for substantial
> amounts of federal aid. (pp. 6–7)

Many parents and students depend on federal financial aid programs to help meet their obligations for payment of tuition and fees. In terms of student financial assistance, the federal government has concentrated its resources in a few primary programs: student and parent loans; Pell Grants; and campus-based programs that include the Supplemental Educational Opportunity Grant, the Perkins Loan, and the work-study program. McPherson and Schapiro (1991) identified four periods of change for federal student aid: (1) from 1965 to 1973 a moderate total of aid, divided between the Guaranteed Student Loan and the campus-based programs, was generally available to students; (2) from 1973 to 1980 the federal aid budget grew and the new Pell Grant program kept relative pace (in percentage terms) with the increasing amount lent through the Guaranteed Student Loan program; (3) from about 1980 through about 1984, Guaranteed Student Loan growth continued to rise significantly while the Pell Grant program and the campus-based programs declined in terms of real growth; (4) "since 1985 [to 1991], the Pell Grant program has grown by 12% and guaranteed loans by 20% in real terms" (p. 27).

The expansion of higher education both in terms of enrollment and purpose has resulted in increased costs.

Additional highly trained faculty, new administrative roles to meet federal and state mandates, high-cost majors in science and technology, and rising student expectations for athletics, activities, and comfort have all been contributing factors. The cost of a college degree has risen steadily, even as federal financial aid has shifted toward loans rather than grants.

Faculty Roles and Challenges

In the 1960s and 1970s, faculty struggled with student protests, sometimes supporting the students' cause and other times either disagreeing in principle or disapproving of the method students chose to register their complaints. Although the level of faculty-student interaction varied significantly depending on the type and size of the institution, the traditional, supervisory role of faculty and administrators ended when the concept of *in loco parentis* declined in favor after 1971. It was in that year that the Twenty-sixth Amendment to the U.S. Constitution was passed which lowered the voting age to eighteen. Students who could vote and could be drafted into military service were not inclined to be carefully supervised on campus any longer. The ability of faculty to interact directly with parents was also diminished with the passage of the **Family Education Rights and Privacy Act** (FERPA) in 1974. Popularly known as the Buckley Amendment, it assured college students' rights to their educational record while limiting access to others.

in loco parentis
refers to the tradition of faculty taking the role of parents in order to guide and discipline students

Family Education Rights and Privacy Act, 1974
protects the privacy of student education records

The primary responsibilities of the faculty have not changed significantly since the mid-1900s and they continue to teach, engage in scholarly activities, and to offer service to the institution and the community. Their many contributions to the rapid expansion of knowledge are highly valued, but they are sometimes criticized for promoting a level of specialization so specific that it creates barriers to interdisciplinary knowledge and understanding. This depth of specialized knowledge requires a substantial commitment of time and energy, but students and parents also demand personalized attention, pressing faculty between expectations for high-quality teaching and institutional requirements for scholarship. The majority of faculty continue to protect and defend the ideals of tenure and academic freedom, and they are especially concerned about the potential response of institutions to the finan-

cial downturn of the early 21st century. At its annual meeting in 2010 the American Association of University Professors censured two institutional administrations for the elimination of faculty positions, including faculty with tenure, following declarations of an enrollment emergency (American Association of University Professors, 2010, "AAUP Censures Two").

In the last quarter of the 20th century, a new instructional format gradually gained acceptance. With the potential to radically change the university, online instruction has continued to grow in popularity. Faculty have generally been hesitant to embrace this teaching and learning methodology and even those who do are often ill-prepared to use it effectively. Jorge Larreamendy-Joerns and Gaea Leinhardt (2006) identify two complementary movements: the merging of online teaching and learning into the mainstream at many institutions and the increasingly significant role distance learning plays. While some faculty welcome it as an effective strategy to overcome the limitations of the classroom, others view it as a threat to the very essence of a quality education. Larreamendy-Joerns and Leinhardt (2006) note that such reactions are not unique to online instruction and that "they occur whenever pedagogical innovations challenge the classroom as the privileged scenario for learning and instruction, and the teacher as the ultimate source of knowledge and control" (p. 572). Whether or not the faculty are prepared, online programs have gained acceptance at many institutions and, with accreditation, the public has developed confidence in them. Clear evidence is provided by enrollment at the University of Phoenix. In fall 2007, with 224,880 students, this fully online institution had, by far, the largest enrollment of any college or university in the country (U.S. Department of Education, n.d., "Which Colleges Have"). It is likely this form of instruction will continue to grow and will, in fact, change the nature of undergraduate life in meaningful ways.

The pressure to assess the quality and effectiveness of higher education has also challenged the academy. Concerns regarding the anticipated loss of academic freedom resulting from the intrusion of non-academics into the life of the classroom are not uncommon. Still, regional and specialized accrediting associations, government agencies,

and to some degree the public began calling more earnestly for accountability in the late 20th century.

Student Life

Student Protest

The 1960s were turbulent times on college campuses as students ardently supported the Civil Rights Movement and actively protested the Vietnam War. The Civil Rights Movement was of primary importance in the early 1960s. Although, in 1954, the U.S. Supreme Court decided that segregated public facilities, including schools, were illegal, insufficient progress toward integration had occurred by the early 1960s. Many institutions, both public and private, remained segregated. As a result, in February 1960 four Black students staged a sit-in at a segregated lunch counter in Greensboro, North Carolina. They were not served and eventually left. However, the next day, a larger group returned and civil rights groups began to organize sit-ins at lunch counters in other stores. The movement spread and soon there were similar protests at segregated churches, beaches, motels, libraries, parks, and theaters. By August 1961, more than 70,000 people had participated in sit-ins and about 3,000 had been arrested for doing so. The non-violent resistance demonstrated by the sit-ins established a model that exemplified the Civil Rights Movement in its early years. **The Student Nonviolent Coordinating Committee** (SNCC) was formed and organized freedom marches and voter registration drives in which both Black and White students participated. Students in the North supported the cause through fund-raising, petitions, and picketing chain stores that discriminated against Blacks (International Civil Rights Center & Museum, n.d.).

Student Nonviolent Coordinating Committee
one of the principal organizations supporting the Civil Rights Movement

Access to equal education at all levels was an important goal of the civil rights agenda. Numerous incidents, many violent, accompanied attempts by Blacks to enroll in public schools historically reserved for Whites. William Doyle (2001) presents a detailed account of the protest that took place when James Meredith, a Black Air Force veteran, attempted to register at the University of Mississippi in 1962 following an order of the U.S. Supreme Court to accept him. Attempting to become the first Black student to enroll, he was physically blocked by the governor, state police, and thousands of White students and citizens. President John F. Kennedy called 30,000 troops into Mississippi to

stop the battle and enforce Meredith's right to attend the university.

In summer 1960, the House Un-American Activities Committee, continuing its work to expose communism, arrived in the San Francisco Bay area. A crowd of about 1,000, including many students from the University of California at Berkeley and San Francisco State College, protested the hearings. They were forcibly removed from the steps of City Hall with fire hoses and several were arrested. The film *Operation Abolition* was produced by the Un-American Activities Committee and distributed in an attempt to place the blame for the disruption on Communist subversives. Over the next few years, continued concern for freedom of speech set the stage for the first major student uprising, which took place at the University of California at Berkeley in fall 1964. At Berkeley, a strip of university property just outside the gate had traditionally afforded individuals a place to pass out pamphlets and solicit students to any cause. The administration decided to enforce a standing (but long-ignored) rule banning use of the strip for off-campus political groups. According to Professor David Burner (1996), the administration became concerned because the activities on the strip were targeting Berkeley itself and area businessmen who practiced discrimination. Demonstrators set up tables on the strip in protest on September 29, 1964 and refused to leave. The names of five protestors were recorded, and they were told to report to university officials the next day to be disciplined. Instead of five students, five hundred reported and demanded equal punishment. Eight students were suspended. The leader of the group, Mario Savio, would become the voice of the **Free Speech Movement**. As students were arriving for classes on October 1st, they were encouraged to stand up against the administration or risk being picked off "one by one." A half dozen or so student groups, including Students for a Democratic Society, the Congress of Racial Equality, and the Student Nonviolent Coordinating Committee, set up tables in front of the administration building. The assistant dean went to one table and asked a young man to identify himself. The young man, Jack Weinberg, refused and the dean ordered police to arrest him. As he was calmly dragged to a waiting car, protestors came to his rescue singing "We Shall Overcome" and surrounding the vehicle. For thirty-two

Free Speech Movement
organized by students at the University of California at Berkeley to secure the right to freedom of speech on campus

hours the car remained stationary, holding Weinberg and his police escort as it was surrounded by protestors. One after another, speakers climbed onto the car and addressed the audience while about one hundred fraternity brothers and athletes threw eggs and lighted cigarettes at them. Finally, an agreement was reached between the president of the University of California, Clark Kerr, and the protestors to form a committee composed of faculty, students, and administrators to consider the issues of campus political behavior and to allow a committee of the academic senate to consider the question of the suspension of the eight students. No charges were pressed against Weinberg. The Free Speech Movement was born and grew, demanding that the First Amendment be the singular guide to political activity on the campus (Burner, 1996, pp. 138–140).

Between 1964 and 1968, national student organizations increased in size and strength as protestors were provoked by civil and legislative punishment or threats of it. Disillusionment with society in general, and especially

Establishment

term used to describe the group holding social, political, and economic power and authority

with the political and social **establishment**, prompted more violent action. Malcolm X was assassinated early in 1965 and later that year racial tension erupted in the Watts neighborhood of Los Angeles. The Watts Riots lasted six days, killed 34, and resulted in the arrest of over 1,000 people. As chairman of the Student Nonviolent Coordinating Committee (SNCC), Stokely Carmichael agreed to expel Whites, including many college students who had previously worked with the SNCC. The fight for civil rights moved to a militant position with the establishment of the Black Panther Party which called for Black separatism and Black power. Demonstrations and violent riots stunned the nation during the 1968 Democratic National Convention in Chicago.

In 1965, the bombing of North Vietnam and the role of university research in the war effort prompted students to view the university itself as a part of the problem. By the end of the 1960s, students were protesting the draft by burning draft cards, interfering with recruiting by the military and representatives of companies that were part of the war industry, and vandalizing or burning university buildings that housed the Reserve Officer Training Corps (ROTC). Anti-war protests attracted hundreds of thousands of demonstrators and spread from the large public universities to many private institutions. The

political system and, in a new twist, the university itself became targets of protests. Both were viewed as part of the same oppressive system. A major demonstration and the occupation of the administration building took place at Columbia University over the institution's plans to displace Black residents of a neighboring ghetto in order to build a new gymnasium. Black students initiated the protest and were joined by members of the Students for a Democratic Society. Five buildings were held for a week before the protest came to an end when city police were summoned. One hundred forty-eight individuals were injured and 707 arrested. At Cornell University, Black student demands for a separate Afro-American studies program and the subsequent burning of a cross in front of a Black women's cooperative resulted in the occupation of Willard Straight Hall. Responding to threats of violence by other students, the protestors received guns from their supporters (Astin, Astin, Bayer, & Bisconti, 1975, pp. 726–730). The protest ended without violence but this incident and others like it were regularly featured on the evening news and reinforced the perception that the campuses were out of control.

The most serious violence occurred in the months following President Richard Nixon's April 1970 announcement of the invasion of Cambodia. The National Guard was called to the Kent State University campus in response to a demonstration and, for reasons that remain unclear, opened fire on students, killing four and wounding nine. Within two weeks, unrest at Jackson State brought the state police, the highway patrol, and the National Guard to campus. Like Kent State, rocks were thrown and officers were taunted but there is no clear and compelling explanation for the action that followed. Gathered around a Jackson State women's residence hall, law enforcement officials opened fire. As a result, two students died and twelve were wounded. All were Black. Then, toward the end of the summer at the University of Wisconsin the building that housed the Army Mathematics Research Center was bombed, killing one, injuring four, and destroying the work of graduate students and professors (Astin, Astin, Bayer, & Bisconti, 1975, pp. 726–730).

In response to the escalating violence, President Nixon appointed a special commission to investigate campus unrest and offer recommendations. Chaired by former

governor of Pennsylvania William W. Scranton, the report cited two components of campus unrest: a crisis of violence and a crisis of understanding. The commissioners wrote:

Campus protest has been focused on three major questions: racial injustice, war, and the university itself.

The first issue is the unfilled promise of full justice and dignity for Blacks and other minorities. Blacks, like many others of different races and ethnic origins, are demanding today that the pledges of the Declaration of Independence and the Emancipation Proclamation be fulfilled now. Full social justice and dignity—an end to racism in all its human, social, and cultural forms—is a central demand of today's students—black, brown, and white.

A great majority of students and a majority of their elders oppose the Indochina war. Many believe it entirely immoral. And if the war is wrong, students insist, then so are all policies and practices that support it, from the draft to military research, from ROTC to recruiting for [the] defense industry. This opposition has led to an ever-widening wave of student protests.

The shortcomings of the American university are the third target of student protest. The goals, values, administration, and curriculum of the modern university have been sharply criticized by many students. Students complain that their studies are irrelevant to the social problems that concern them. They want to shape their own personal and common lives, but find the university restrictive. They seek a community of companions and scholars, but find an impersonal multiversity. And they denounce the university's relationship to the war and the discriminatory racial practices.

Behind the student protest on these issues and the crisis of violence to which they have contributed lies the more basic crisis of understanding.

Americans have never shared a single culture, a single philosophy, or a single religion. But in most periods of our history, we have shared many common values, common sympathies, and a common dedication to a system of government which protects our diversity.

We are now in grave danger of losing what is common among us through growing intolerance of opposing views on issues and of diversity itself.

A "new" culture is emerging primarily among students. Membership is often manifested by differences in dress and life style. Most of its members have high ideals and great fears. They stress the need for humanity, equality, and the sacredness of life. They fear that nuclear war will make them the last generation in history. They

see their elders as entrapped by materialism and competition, and as prisoners of outdated social forms. They believe their own country has lost its sense of human purpose. They see the Indochina war as an onslaught by a technological giant upon the peasant people of a small, harmless, and backward nation. The war is seen as draining resources from the urgent needs of social and racial justice. They argue that we are the first nation with sufficient resources to create not only decent lives for some, but a decent society for all, and that we are failing to do so. They feel we must remake America in its own image.

But among members of this new student culture, there is a growing lack of tolerance, a growing insistence that their own views must govern, an impatience with the slow procedures of a liberal democracy, a growing denial of the humanity and good will of those who urge patience and restraint, and particularly of those whose duty it is to enforce the law. A small number, not terrorists themselves, would not turn even arsonists and bombers over to law enforcement officials.

At the same time, many Americans have reacted to this emerging culture with an intolerance of their own. They reject not only that which is impatient, unrestrained, and intolerant in the new culture of the young, but even that which is good. Worse, they reject the individual members of the student culture themselves. Distinctive dress alone is enough to draw insult and abuse. Increasing numbers of citizens believe that students who dissent or protest—even those who protest peacefully—deserve to be treated harshly. Some even say that when dissenters are killed, they have brought death upon themselves. Less and less do students and the larger community seek to understand or respect the viewpoint and motivations of others.

If this trend continues, if this crisis of understanding endures, the very survival of the nation will be threatened. A nation driven to use weapons of war upon its youth is a nation on the edge of chaos. A nation that has lost the allegiance of part of its youth is a nation that has lost its future. A nation whose young have become intolerant of diversity, intolerant of the rest of its citizenry, and intolerant of all traditional values simply because they are traditional has no generation worthy or capable of assuming leadership in the years to come. (Commission on Campus Unrest, 1970, pp. 3–5)

The commissioners captured the sense that, for many Americans during this period regardless of position or perspective, the country seemed to be breaking apart.

Student Enrollment

Martin Trow (1974) described three phases of higher education in relation to the development of a system of higher education. The first, elite higher education, prepares the elite members of the ruling class for positions of leadership and power through the shaping of the mind and the development of character. The second, mass higher education, shifts emphasis from shaping character to the acquisition of skills for elite, technical roles. The third, universal higher education, attempts to prepare large numbers (not primarily elites) for life in a society marked by rapid technical and social change.

In 1960, roughly 40% of all secondary school seniors were accepted into college and that percentage rose to 52% in 1970 and to 61% in 1991. The United States now maintains a system that offers universal access, serving well over 50% of the 18- to 21-year-old age cohort. Public institutions absorbed much of the enrollment growth that took place between the 1970s and the 1990s (Lucas, 2006, pp. 248–249). There were about 11.2 million undergraduate students in higher education in the fall 1986. Approximately half were enrolled as full-time students, attending the full academic year. Approximately 80% of them were traditional age (23 years old or younger) and 38% of the total enrollment was at four-year public colleges and universities. Private four-year colleges and universities enrolled about 17% of the total, 38% were in programs of two years or less at public colleges, 1% were at private colleges with programs of two years or less, and about 5% were at proprietary institutions in vocational or technical programs, most of which were two years or less in duration (McPherson & Schapiro, 1991, p. 3).

Enrollment trends at the undergraduate, graduate, and first-professional levels have varied. During the 1970s, undergraduate enrollment generally increased but dropped from 10.8 million to 10.6 million between 1983 and 1985. It increased each year from 1985 to 1992, rising 18% before declining 2% and then stabilizing between 1993 and 1996. Between 1997 and 2007, undergraduate enrollment rose 25%. During the late 1970s and early 1980s, graduate enrollment was relatively consistent at about 1.3 million, but between 1985 and 2007 it rose about 67%. Enrollment in first-professional programs rose 60% between 1970 and 1980 and then stabilized in the 1980s. Enrollment in first-

professional programs began rising again in the 1990s, increasing 18% between 1997 and 2007 (U.S. Department of Education, 2009, "College Enrollment," para. 3).

Overall enrollment, including enrollment of female students and students from traditionally underrepresented groups, increased during the last several decades of the 20th century. According to the National Center for Education Statistics (NCES):

> Enrollment in degree-granting institutions increased by 14 percent between 1987 and 1997. Between 1997 and 2007, enrollment increased at a faster rate (26 percent), from 14.5 million to 18.2 million. Much of the growth between 1997 and 2007 was in full-time enrollment; the number of full-time students rose 34 percent, while the number of part-time students rose 15 percent. During the same time period, the number of females rose 29 percent, compared to an increase of 22 percent in the number of males. Enrollment increases can be affected both by population growth and by rising rates of enrollment. Between 1997 and 2007, the number of 18- to 24-year-olds increased from 25.5 million to 29.5 million, an increase of 16 percent, and the percentage of 18- to 24-year-olds enrolled in college remained relatively stable (37 percent in 1997 and 39 percent in 2007).
>
> The number of young students has been growing more rapidly than the number of older students, but this pattern is expected to shift. Between 1995 and 2006, the enrollment of students under age 25 increased by 33 percent. Enrollment of people 25 and over rose by 13 percent during the same period. From 2006 to 2017, NCES projects a rise of 10 percent in enrollments of people under 25, and a rise of 19 percent in enrollments of people 25 and over.
>
> The percentage of American college students who are minorities has been increasing. In 1976, 15 percent were minorities, compared with 32 percent in 2007. Much of the change from 1976 to 2007 can be attributed to rising numbers of Hispanic and Asian or Pacific Islander students. During that time period, the percentage of Asian or Pacific Islander students rose from 2 percent to 7 percent and the Hispanic percentage rose from 4 percent to 11 percent. The percentage of Black students was 9 percent at the beginning of the time period and it fluctuated during the early part of the period before rising to 13 percent in 2007. Nonresident aliens for whom race/ethnicity is not reported made up 3 percent of the total enrollment in 2007. (U.S. Department of Education, 2009, "College Enrollment," paras. 1, 2, 5)

Conclusion

In 1987, the Carnegie Foundation for the Advancement of Teaching sponsored a report on undergraduate education in the United States. Ernest L. Boyer (1987) conducted the investigation and identified eight "points of tension" which "appeared with such regularity and seemed so consistently to sap the vitality of the undergraduate experience" that they were the focus of the report (p. 2). Those eight points were:

1. The transition from school to college: disconnect between college and the earlier levels of education;
2. The goals and curriculum of education: colleges seem confused about their mission; the disciplines are fragmented and undergraduates find it difficult to make connections; student focus is on career preparation;
3. The priorities of the faculty: comparative relationships between teaching and scholarship;
4. The condition of teaching and learning: tension between conformity and creativity in the classroom;
5. The quality of campus life: disconnect between academic and social life on campus;
6. The governance of the college: declining confidence in decision-making process on campus;
7. Assessing outcomes: assessment of college goals linked to evaluation of student achievement;
8. The connection between the campus and the world: intellectual and social isolation separating the college from the world. (Boyer, 1987, pp. 2–6)

Boyer (1987), wisely acknowledging that these problems are not new but "in one way or another, have troubled higher education for generations" (p. 6), encouraged institutions to think of them as presenting an opportunity for a constructive debate about the meaning of the undergraduate college and to consider ways to make the experience more vital and enriching.

There are critics of American higher education who believe the academy has lost its way. They cite the lack of integrity in the undergraduate experience, the focus on research rather than teaching, and the career orientation of some majors at the expense of the liberal arts. Perhaps most challenging is the question of purpose. Higher education is expected to produce an "educated" person, yet there is not a clear and common definition of such a person.

In colonial times, a college graduate understood Latin and Greek, he could read the classics and, whether he agreed or not, had learned about the relationship between God and man from a Christian perspective. Through a relatively homogeneous curriculum, he was prepared for the ministry or public life but could readily function in business or another professional role. As an educated man, he had learned all that was needed to preserve the culture of his time and to be very successful in the society in which he lived. In the 21st century, given the tremendous expansion of knowledge, cultural diversity, globalization, rapidly changing technologies, myriad employment possibilities, and continuing questions of human purpose, what is the educational equivalent today?

The majority of students who began college in fall 2010 as traditional freshmen were born in 1991 or 1992, just about the time the World Wide Web was created. They are comfortable with technology as a common element of their lifestyle. Theirs is the age of information and they have been raised in an environment of instant communication with immediate access to seemingly infinite resources on the Internet. As they, and the cohorts that will follow them, experience higher education, institutions will be required to seamlessly incorporate technology in revolutionary new ways.

Expanding access, evolving technologies, demographic shifts, social change, economic realities, and new national priorities will shape higher education in the future just as similar issues have influenced its development. At this point, the early part of the 21st century, the pressure on the American system of higher education is strong, the challenges are many, and the potential for innovative evolution is tremendous.

GLOSSARY

Civil Rights Act of 1964: outlawed segregation in businesses and banned discrimination in employment and public places

Civil Rights Movement: organized effort to secure civil rights, primarily through nonviolent means

Elementary and Secondary Education Act, 1965: legislated sweeping education reform aimed at elementary and secondary levels

Higher Education Act of 1965: focused on improving postsecondary education and provided significant financial aid for students

No Child Left Behind Act of 2001: reauthorization of the Elementary and Secondary Education Act intended to increase accountability and transparency

in loco parentis: refers to the tradition of faculty taking the role of parents in order to guide and discipline students

Family Education Rights and Privacy Act, 1974: protects the privacy of student education records

Student Nonviolent Coordinating Committee: one of the principal organizations supporting the Civil Rights Movement

Free Speech Movement: organized by students at the University of California at Berkeley to secure the right to freedom of speech on campus

Establishment: term used to describe the group holding social, political, and economic power and authority

References
and Resources

References

Altschuler, G. C., & Blumin, S. M. (2009). *The G.I. bill: A new deal for veterans*. New York: Oxford University Press.

American Association of University Professors. (1915). *General declaration of principles*. Retrieved from http://www.aaup.org/AAUP/pubsres/policydocs/contents/1915.htm

American Association of University Professors. (1940). *Statement of principles on academic freedom and tenure*. Retrieved from http://www.aaup.org/AAUP/pubsres/policydocs/contents/1940statement.htm

American Association of University Professors. (2010). *AAUP censures two administrations and sanctions one*. Retrieved from http://www.aaup.org/AAUP/newsroom/2010PRS/censure.htm

Anderson, J. D. (1988). *The education of Blacks in the South, 1860–1935*. Chapel Hill:

Astin, A.W., Astin, H. S., Bayer, A. E., & Bisconti, A. S. (1975). Overview of the unrest era. Reprinted in L. F. Goodchild & H. S. Wechsler (Eds.). (1997). *The history of higher education* (2nd ed.) (pp. 724–738). Needham Heights, MA: Simon & Schuster.

Barnard. (n.d.). A brief history. Retrieved from http://www.barnard.edu/about/history.htm

Boyer, E. L. (1987). *College: The undergraduate experience in America*. New York: Harper & Row.

Brint, S., & Karabel, J. (1989). *The diverted dream: Community colleges and the promise of educational opportunity in America, 1900–1985.* New York: Oxford University Press.

Brittingham, B. (2009). Accreditation in the United States: How did we get where we are? In P.M. O'Brien, S. N. D. (Ed.), *Accreditation: Ensuring and enhancing quality. New Directions for Higher Education, 145* (pp. 7–27). San Francisco, CA: Jossey-Bass.

Brown University. (n.d.). About Brown. Retrieved from http://www.brown.edu/web/about/history

Brown v. the Board of Education of Topeka, 347 U.S. 483 (1954).

Brubacher, J. S., & Rudy, W. (1976). *Higher education in transition: A history of American colleges and universities, 1636–1976.* New York: Harper & Row.

Bryn Mawr. (n.d.). A brief history of Bryn Mawr. Retrieved from http://www.brynmawr.edu/character/history.shtml

Buetow, H. A. (1970). *Of singular benefit.* New York: Macmillan.

Burner, D. (1996). *Making peace with the 60s.* Princeton, NJ: Princeton University Press.

Burns, J. A. (1937). *A history of Catholic education in the United States: A textbook for normal schools and teachers' colleges.* New York: Benziger Brothers.

Carnegie Foundation for the Advancement of Teaching. (n.d.). Carnegie classification of institutions of higher education. Retrieved from http://classifications.carnegiefoundation.org/

Chronicle of Higher Education. (c2010a). Carnegie classification of institutions of higher education. Reprinted with permission. Retrieved from http://chronicle.com/article/2005-Carnegie-Classificatio/47991/

Chronicle of Higher Education. (c2010b). Degrees awarded by type of institution, 2006–2007. Reprinted with permission. Retrieved from http://chronicle.com/article/Degrees-Awarded-by-Type-of-/48040/

Chronicle of Higher Education Almanac. (c2010c). Number of full-time faculty members by sex, rank, and racial and ethnic group, fall 2007. Reprinted with permission. Retrieved from http://chronicle.com/article/Number-of-Full-Time-Faculty/47992/

Church, R. L., & Sedlak, M. W. (1976). *Education in the United States: An interpretive history.* New York: The Free Press.

Civil Rights Restoration Act of 1987. (1988). Retrieved from http://www.fhwa.dot.gov/environment/ejustice/facts/restoration_act.htm

Cohen, A. M. (1998). *The shaping of American higher education: Emergence and growth of the contemporary system.* San Francisco: Jossey-Bass.

Cohen, A. M., & Brawer, F. B. (2008). *The American community college* (5th ed.). San Francisco: Jossey-Bass.

Columbia University. (n.d.). A brief history. Retrieved from http://www.columbia.edu/about_columbia/history.html

Commission on Campus Unrest. (1970). *Report of the President's Commission on Campus Unrest.* Washington, D.C.: U.S. Government Printing Office.

Congressional Quarterly Service. (1967). *Federal role in education* (2nd ed.). Washington, D.C.: CQ Press: A Division of Sage Publications, Inc.

Council for Aid to Education. (2009). *Voluntary support for education*. New York: Author.

Cremin, L. A. (1970). *American education: The colonial experience, 1607–1783*. New York: Harper & Row.

Dartmouth University. (n.d.). History. Retrieved from http://www.dartmouth.edu/home/about/history.html

Doyle, W. (2001). *An American insurrection: The battle of Oxford, Mississippi*. New York: Doubleday.

Eddy, E. D. (1957). *Colleges for our land and time: The land-grant idea in American education*. New York: Harper & Brothers.

Falla, J. (1981). *NCAA: The voice of college sports: A diamond anniversary history, 1906–1981*. Mission, KS: National Collegiate Athletic Association.

Finkelstein, M. (1983). From tutor to specialized scholar: Academic professionalization in eighteenth and nineteenth century America. Reprinted in L. F. Goodchild & H. S. Wechsler (Eds.). (1997). *The history of higher education* (2nd ed.) (pp. 80–93). Needham Heights, MA: Simon & Schuster.

Goodchild, L. F. (1986). The turning point in American Jesuit education: The standardization controversy between the Jesuits and the North Central Association, 1915–1940. Reprinted in L. F. Goodchild & H. S. Wechsler (Eds.). (1997). *The history of higher education* (2nd ed.), (pp. 528–550). Needham Heights, MA: Simon & Schuster.

Gordon, L. D. (1990). *Gender and higher education in the Progressive Era*. New Haven, CT: Yale University Press.

Gruber, C. S. (1975). *Mars and Minerva: World War I and the uses of higher learning in America*. Baton Rouge: Louisiana State University Press.

Harper, C. (1939). *A century of public teacher education: The story of the state teachers colleges as they evolved from the normal schools*. Washington, D.C.: Hugh Birch–Horace Mann Fund for the American Association of Teachers Colleges.

Harvard Charter of 1650. (1650). Retrieved from the Harvard University Archives Web site: http://hul.harvard.edu/huarc/charter.html

Hofstadter, R. & Hardy, C. D. (1952). *The development and scope of higher education in the United States*. New York: Columbia University Press.

Hofstadter, R., & Metzger, W. P. (1955). *The development of academic freedom in the United States*. New York: Columbia University Press.

Horowitz, H. L. (1984). *Alma mater: Design and experience in the women's colleges from their nineteenth-century beginnings to the 1930s*. New York: Knopf.

International Civil Rights Center & Museum. (n.d.). The Greensboro chronology. Retrieved from http://www.sitinmovement.org/history/greensboro-chronology.asp

Jackson, C. L., & Nunn, E. F. (2003). *Historically Black colleges and universities: A reference handbook*. Santa Barbara, CA: ABC-CLIO.

Johnson, E. L. (1981). Misconceptions about the early land-grant colleges. *The Journal of Higher Education, 52*(4), 333–351.

Johnson, W. R. (1989). Teachers and teacher training in the twentieth century. In D. Warren (Ed.), *American teachers: Histories of a profession at work* (pp. 237–256). New York: Macmillan.

Kennelly, K. (2002). Faculties and what they taught. In T. Schier & C. Russett (Eds.), *Catholic women's colleges in America* (pp. 98–122). Baltimore: Johns Hopkins University Press.

Kerber, L. (1980). *Women of the Republic: Intellect and ideology in Revolutionary America*. Chapel Hill: University of North Carolina Press.

Lapchick, R. E., & Slaughter, J. B. (1994). *The rules of the game: Ethics in college sports*. Phoenix, AZ: Oryx Press.

Larreamendy-Joerns, J., & Leinhardt, G. (2006). Going the distance with online education. *Review of Educational Research, 76*(4), 567–605.

Lemann, N. (1999). *The big test: The secret history of the American meritocracy*. New York: Farrar, Straus & Giroux.

Liptak, D., R.S.M (1988, c1989). *Immigrants and their church*. New York: Macmillan.

List of the 107 land-grant institutions in the United States and its territories. In L. F. Goodchild & H. S. Wechsler (Eds.). (1997). *The history of higher education* (2nd ed.) (pp. 363–364). Needham Heights, MA: Simon & Schuster.

Lord, J. K. (1913). *History of Dartmouth College, 1815–1909*. Concord, NH: Rumford.

Lucas, C. J. (2006). *American higher education: A history* (2nd ed.). New York: Palgrave Macmillan.

Mahoney, K. A. (2002). American Catholic colleges for women. In T. Schier & C. Russett (Eds.), *Catholic women's colleges in America* (pp. 25–54). Baltimore: Johns Hopkins University Press.

Mahoney, K. A. (2003). *Catholic higher education in Protestant America: The Jesuits and Harvard in the age of the university*. Baltimore: Johns Hopkins University Press.

McConaghy, M., Silberman, M., & Kalashnikova, I. (2004). *Penn in the 18th century*. Retrieved from http://www.archives.upenn.edu/histy/features/1700s/penn1700s.html

McPherson, J. M. (1982). *Ordeal by fire: The Civil War and the reconstruction*. New York: Knopf.

McPherson, M. S., & Schapiro, M. O. (1991). *Keeping college affordable: Government and educational opportunity*. Washington, D.C.: The Brookings Institute.

Medsker, L. L. (1960). *The junior college: Progress and prospect*. New York: McGraw-Hill.

Miller, E.W., & Miller, R. M. (1996). *United States immigration: A reference handbook*. Santa Barbara, CA: ABC-CLIO.

Morrison, S. E. (1936). *Three centuries of Harvard, 1636–1936*. Cambridge, MA: Harvard University Press.

Mount Holyoke. (n.d.). History. Retrieved from http://www.mtholyoke.edu/cic/about/history.shtml

NACUBO and Commonfund Institute. (2010). *2009 NACUBO–Commonfund study of endowments: U.S. and Canadian institutions listed by fiscal year 2009 endowment market value and percentage*. Retrieved from http://www.nacubo.org/Documents/research/2009_NCSE_Public_Tables_Endowment_Market_Values.pdf

National Commission on Excellence in Education. (1983). *A nation at risk: The imperative for educational reform*. Retrieved from http://www2. ed.gov/pubs/NatAtRisk/title.html

Newcomer, M. (1959). *A century of higher education for women*. New York: Harper & Brothers.

Olson, K. W. (1974). *The G.I. bill, the veterans, and the colleges*. Lexington: University Press of Kentucky.

Palinchak, R. S. (1973). *The evolution of the community college*. Metuchen, NJ: Scarecrow Press.

Pfnister, A. O. (1959). *Accreditation in the north central region*. In L. E. Blauch (Ed.), *Accreditation in higher education* (pp. 52–58). Washington, D.C.: U.S. Department of Health, Education, and Welfare.

Potter, D. (1944). *Debating in the colonial chartered colleges: An historical survey, 1642 to 1900*. New York: Teachers College, Columbia University.

Potts, D. B. (1977). "College enthusiasm!" as public response: 1800–1860. *Harvard Educational Review, 47*(1), 28–42.

Power, E. J. (1958). *A history of Catholic education in the United States*. Milwaukee, WI: Bruce.

Power, E. J. (1972). *Catholic higher education in America, a history*. New York: Meredith Corporation.

President's Commission on Higher Education. (1947). *Higher education for American democracy*. New York: Harper & Row.

Princeton University. (n.d.). The presidents of Princeton. Retrieved from http://www.princeton.edu/pr/facts/presidents/

Radcliffe Institute for Advanced Study. (n.d.). *Significant dates in Radcliffe's history*. Retrieved from http://www.radcliffe.edu/about/dates.aspx

Reynolds, J. W. (1965). *The junior college*. New York: The Center for Applied Research in Education.

Ringenberg, W. C. (1984). *The Christian college: A history of Protestant higher education in America*. Grand Rapids, MI: Christian University Press.

Robson, D. W. (1985). *Educating Republicans: The college in the era of the American Revolution, 1750–1800*. Westport, CT: Greenwood.

Roebuck, J. B., & Murty, K. S. (1993). *Historically Black colleges and universities: Their place in American higher education*. Westport, CT: Praeger.

Rudolph, F. (1962). *The American college and university*. New York: Knopf.

Rudolph, F. (1977). *Curriculum: A history of the American undergraduate course of study since 1636*. San Francisco: Jossey-Bass.

Rutgers University. (n.d.). A brief history. Retrieved from http://www. rutgers.edu/about-rutgers/brief-history

Sanders, J. B. (1959). Evolution of accreditation. In L. E. Blauch (Ed.), *Accreditation in higher education* (pp. 9–14). Washington, D.C.: U.S. Department of Health, Education, and Welfare.

Sanders, J. B. (1959). The United States office of education and accreditation. In L. E. Blauch (Ed.), *Accreditation in higher education* (pp. 15–21). Washington, D.C.: U.S. Department of Health, Education, and Welfare.

Savage, H. J., Bentley, H. W., McGovern, J. T., & Smiley, D. F. (1929). *American college athletics.* New York: Carnegie Foundation for the Advancement of Teaching.

Selden, W. K. (1959). The national commission on accrediting. In L. E. Blauch (Ed.), *Accreditation in higher education* (pp. 22–30). Washington, D.C.: U.S. Department of Health, Education, and Welfare.

Selden, W. K. (1960). *Accreditation: A struggle over standards in higher education.* New York: Harper & Brothers.

Sheldon, H. D. (1901). *Student life and customs.* New York: D. Appleton.

Smith College. (n.d.). Smith tradition. Retrieved from http://www.smith.edu/about_smithtradition.php

Solomon, B. M. (1985). *In the company of educated women.* New Haven, CT: Yale University Press.

Statutes of Harvard. (1646). Reprinted in L. F. Goodchild & H. S. Wechsler (Eds.). (1997). *The history of higher education* (2nd ed.) (pp. 125–126). Needham Heights, MA: Simon & Schuster.

Stewart, G. C., Jr. (1994). *Marvels of charity: History of American sisters and nuns.* Huntington, IN: Our Sunday Visitor Publishing Division.

Stewart, G. R. (1950). *The year of the oath: The fight for academic freedom at the University of California.* Garden City, NY: Doubleday.

Tewksbury, D. G. (1932). *The founding of American colleges and universities before the Civil War.* New York: Teachers College, Columbia University.

Thelin, J. R. (2004). *A history of American higher education.* Baltimore: Johns Hopkins University Press.

Thwing, C. (1900). *College administration.* New York: The Century Company.

Title IX, Education Amendments of 1972. (1972). Retrieved from http://www.dol.gov/oasam/regs/statutes/titleix.htm

Torbenson, C. L. (2005). The origin and evolution of college fraternities and sororities. In T. L. Brown, G. S. Parks, & C. M. Phillips (Eds.), *African American fraternities and sororities: The legacy and the vision* (pp. 37–66). Lexington: University Press of Kentucky.

Trivett, D. A. (1976). *Accreditation and institutional eligibility.* ERIC/ Higher Education Research Report No. 9. ERIC Document #132 919. Washington, D.C.: American Association for Higher Education.

Trow, M. (1974). Problems in the transition from elite to mass higher education. In *General Report on the Conference on Future Structures of Post-Secondary Education* (pp. 55–101). Paris: OECD.

Trustees of Dartmouth College v. Woodward, 17 U.S. (4 Wheat.) 518 (1819).

United States Military Academy. (n.d.). A brief history of West Point. Retrieved from http://www.usma.edu/history.asp

University of Virginia. (n.d.). Short history of U.Va. Retrieved from http://www.virginia.edu/uvatours/shorthistory/times.html

University of Wisconsin–Madison. (n.d.). History of the Wisconsin idea. Retrieved from http://www.wisconsinidea.wisc.edu/history.html

U.S. Census Bureau. (2010). "1800 Fast Facts." Retrieved from http://www.census.gov/history/www/through_the_decades/fast_facts/1800_fast_facts.html

U.S. Census Bureau (2010). "1900 Fast Facts." Retrieved from http://www.census.gov/history/www/through_the_decades/fast_facts/1900_fast_facts.html

U.S. Census Bureau. (2010). The 2010 statistical abstract: Education: Higher education: Institutions and enrollment. *#270 College enrollment by selected characteristics.* Retrieved from http://www.census.gov/compendia/statab/cats/education/higher_education_institutions_and_enrollment.html

U.S. Census Bureau. (2010). The 2010 statistical abstract: Education: Higher education: Institutions and enrollment. *#272 college enrollment by sex, age, race, and Hispanic origin: 1980 to 2007.* Retrieved from http://www.census.gov/compendia/statab/cats/education/higher_education_institutions_and_enrollment.html

U.S. Census Bureau. (2010). The 2010 statistical abstract: Education: Higher education: Degrees. *#291 bachelor's degrees earned by field.* Retrieved from http://www.census.gov/compendia/statab/cats/education/higher_education_degrees.html

U.S. Census Bureau. (2010). The 2010 statistical abstract: Education: Higher education: Degrees. *#292 master's and doctorate degrees earned by field.* Retrieved from http://www.census.gov/compendia/statab/cats/education/higher_education_degrees.html

U.S. Department of Education. (2006). *A test of leadership: Charting the future of U.S. higher education.* Washington, D.C.: Author.

U.S. Department of Education, National Center for Education Statistics. (2009). *College enrollment.* Retrieved from http://nces.ed.gov/fastfacts/display.asp?id=98

U.S. Department of Education, National Center for Education Statistics. (n.d.). Table 331: Average undergraduate tuition and fees and room and board rates charged for full-time students in degree-granting institutions, by type and control of institution: 2007–08. Retrieved from http://nces.ed.gov/programs/digest/d08/tables/dt08_331.asp

U.S. Department of Education, National Center for Education Statistics. (n.d.). *What is the average income for high school and college graduates?* Retrieved from http://nces.ed.gov/fastfacts/display.asp?id=77

U.S. Department of Education, National Center for Education Statistics. (n.d.). *Which colleges have the highest enrollment?* Retrieved from http://nces.ed.gov/fastfacts/display.asp?id=74

U.S. Department of the Interior, National Park Service. (n.d.). *Women's rights, declaration of sentiments.* Retrieved from http://www.nps.gov/wori/historyculture/declaration-of-sentiments.htm

Van Rensselaer, S. (1824). Personal correspondence. Retrieved from Rensselaer Polytechnic Institute Archives Web site: http://www.lib.rpi.edu/dept/library/html/Archives/early_documents/svr_letter_transcription.html

Vassar Admissions. (n.d.). History. Retrieved from http://admissions.vassar.edu/about_history.html

Veysey, L. R. (1965). *The emergence of the American university.* Chicago: University of Chicago Press.

Wei, C. C., Berkner, L., He, S., Lew, S., Cominole, M., & Siegel, P. (2009). *2007–08 National Postsecondary Student Aid Study (NPSAS: 08):*

Student financial aid estimates for 2007–08: First look (NCES 2009–166). National Center for Education Statistics. Institute of Education Sciences. U.S. Department of Education. Retrieved from http://www.nces.ed.gov/pubs2009/2009166.pdf

Wellesley College. (n.d.). Wellesley College history. Retrieved from http://web.wellesley.edu/web/AboutWellesley/CollegeHistory

Whitehead, J. S., & Herbst, J. (1986). How to think about the Dartmouth College case. *History of Education Quarterly, 26*(3), pp. 333–349.

Wilberforce University. (n.d.). History. Retrieved from http://www.wilberforce.edu/welcome/history.html

William & Mary. (n.d.). The Indian school at William & Mary. Retrieved from http://www.wm.edu/about/history/historiccampus/indianschool/index.php

Woody, T. (1929). *A history of women's education in the United States* (Vols. 1–2). New York: Science Press.

Wright, B. (1988). "For the children of infidels?" American Indian education in the colonial colleges. *American Indian Culture and Research Journal, 12*(3), pp. 1–14.

Yale Report. (1828). Reprinted in L. F. Goodchild & H. S. Wechsler (Eds.). (1997). *The history of higher education* (2nd ed.) (pp. 191–199). Needham Heights, MA: Simon & Schuster.

Yale University. (n.d.). About Yale. Retrieved from http://www.yale.edu/about/history.html

Additional Resources

Alexander, S. D. (1872). *Princeton College during the eighteenth century.* New York: Anson D. F. Randolph.

Alstete, J. W. (2004). Accreditation matters: Achieving academic recognition and renewal. *ERIC-ASHE Higher Education Report (30)*4. Hoboken, NJ: Wiley Periodicals.

Altbach, P. G., Berdahl, R. O., & Gumport, P. J. (1999). *American higher education in the twenty-first century: Social, political, and economic challenges.* Baltimore: Johns Hopkins University Press.

American Council on Education. (1970). Campus tensions: Analysis and recommendations. In *Report of the special committee on campus tensions.* Washington, DC: Author.

Berlin, I. (1974). *Slaves without masters: The free Negro in the antebellum South.* New York: Pantheon Books.

Bloom, A. D. (1987). *The closing of the American mind.* New York: Simon & Schuster.

Boland, H. G. (2001). *Creating the Council for Higher Education Accreditation (CHEA).* Phoenix, AZ: The American Council on Education and the Oryx Press.

Boorstin, D. J. (1960, c1948). *The lost world of Thomas Jefferson.* Boston: Beacon Press.

Bowen, J. (1972). *A history of western education* (Vols. 1–3). New York: St. Martin's.

Brewer, E. M. (1987). *Nuns and the education of American Catholic women.* Chicago: Loyola University Press.

Brick, M. (1964). *Forum and focus for the community college movement*. New York: Teachers College, Columbia University.

Burns, J. A. (1912). *The growth and development of the Catholic school system in the United States*. New York: Benziger Brothers.

Carrell, W. (1968). American college professors: 1750–1800. *History of Education Quarterly, 8*, 289–305.

Cremin, L.A. (1977). *Traditions of American education*. New York: Basic Books.

Cremin, L.A. (1980). *American education, the national experience, 1783–1876*. New York: Harper & Row.

Flattau, P. E., Bracken, J., Van Atta, R., Bandeh-Ahmadi, A., de la Cruz, R., & Sullivan, K. (2007). *The National Defense Education Act of 1958: Selected outcomes*. Washington, DC: Science & Technology Policy Institute.

Foner, E. (1988). *America's unfinished revolution, 1873–1877*. New York: Harper & Row.

Goodchild, L. F., & Wechsler, H. S. (Eds). (1997). *The history of higher education* (2nd ed.). Needham Heights, MA: Simon & Schuster.

Herbst, J. (1973). *The history of American education*. Northbrook, IL: AHM.

Herbst, J. (1982). *From crisis to crisis: American college government, 1636–1819*. Cambridge, MA: Harvard University Press.

Herbst, J. (1989). *And sadly teach: Teacher education and professionalization in American culture*. Madison: University of Wisconsin Press.

Hawkins, H. (1992). *Banding together: The rise of national associations in higher education, 1887–1950*. Baltimore: Johns Hopkins University Press.

Hobbs, W. C. (Ed.). (1978). *Government regulation of higher education*. Cambridge, MA: Ballinger.

Hoeveler, J. D. (2002). *Creating the American mind: Intellect and politics in the colonial colleges*. New York: Rowman & Littlefield.

Hofstadter, R., & Smith, W. (1961). *American higher education: A documentary history* (Vols. 1–2). Chicago: University of Chicago Press.

Kendell, E. (1976). *"Peculiar institutions": An informal history of the Seven Sister colleges*. New York: Putnam.

Koos, L. (1925). *The junior-college movement*. Boston: Ginn.

McCormack, A. C., & Zhao, C.-M. (2005). Rethinking and reframing the Carnegie Classification, *Change, 37*(5), 50–57. Retrieved from http://www.carnegiefoundation.org/elibrary/rethinking-and-reframing-carnegie-classification

Miller, A. (1976). *A college in dispersion: Women of Bryn Mawr 1896–1975*. Boulder, CO: Westview Press.

Morrill Act of 1862. Retrieved from http://www.ourdocuments.gov/doc.php?flash=true&doc=33&page=transcript

Orlans, H. (1962). *The effects of federal programs on higher education: A study of 36 universities and colleges*. Washington, DC: The Brookings Institution.

Oviatt, E. (1916). *The beginnings of Yale, 1701–1726*. New Haven, CT: Yale University Press.

Parker, A. B. (1902). Rights of donors. *Educational Review, 23*, 19–21.

Parks, G. S. (2008). *Black Greek-letter organizations in the 21st century: Our fight has just begun.* Lexington: University Press of Kentucky.

Quincy, J. (1840). *The history of Harvard University.* Cambridge, MA: J. Owen.

Russell, J. E. (1951). *Federal activities in higher education after the Second World War.* New York: King's Crown.

Schrecker, E. W. (1986). *No ivory tower: McCarthyism and the universities.* New York: Oxford University Press.

Shores, L. (1934). *Origins of the American college library.* Nashville, TN: Cullom & Ghertner.

Thwing, C. F. (1883). *American colleges: Their students and work.* New York: G. P. Putnam's Sons.

Thwing, C. F. (1906). *A history of higher education in America.* New York: D. Appleton.

Thwing, C. F. (1914). *The American college: What it is and what it may become.* New York: Platt & Peck.

Thwing, C. F. (1920). *The American colleges and universities in the Great War, 1914–1919: A history.* New York: Macmillan.

Veblen, T. (1918). *The higher learning in America: A memorandum on the conduct of universities by business men.* New York: Viking.

Vine, P. (1976). The social function of eighteenth century higher education. *History of Education Quarterly, 16*(4), 409–424.

Warren, D. (Ed.). (1989). *American teachers: Histories of a profession at work.* New York: Macmillan.

Willie, C. V., & Edmonds, R. R. (1978). *Black colleges in America: Challenge, development, survival.* New York: Teachers College, Columbia University.

Relevant Web sites

American Association of Colleges for Teacher Education
www.aacte.org

American Association of Collegiate Registrars and Admissions Officers
http://www.aacrao.org

American Association of University Professors
www.aaup.org/

American College Personnel Association
http://www2.myacpa.org

American Educational Research Association
www.aera.net

Association for the Study of Higher Education
www.ashe.ws

Association of Catholic Colleges and Universities
http://www.accunet.org/i4a/pages/index.cfm?pageid=1

Association of Jesuit Colleges and Universities
http://www.ajcunet.edu/

Carnegie Foundation for the Advancement of Teaching
www.carnegiefoundation.org/

Chronicle of Higher Education
  http://chronicle.com/section/Home/5
College Entrance Examination Board
  www.collegeboard.com
College Student Educators International
  http://www2.myacpa.org/
Council for Higher Education Accreditation
  www.chea.org
Middle States Association of Colleges and Schools
  http://www.middlestates.or
National Association for Accreditation of Teacher Education
New England Association of Schools and Colleges
  http://www.neasc.org
National Association for Equal Opportunity in Higher Education
  www.nafeo.org
National Association of College and University Business Officers
  http://www.nacubo.org/
National Association of University Women
  www.nauw1910.org/
National Center for Education Statistic
  http://nces.ed.gov/
National Collegiate Athletic Association
  http://www.ncaa.org/
No Child Left Behind
  http://www2.ed.gov/nclb/
North Central Association of Colleges and Schools
  http://www.northcentralassociation.org
Northwest Association of Secondary and Higher School
  http://www.neccu.org
Publications of the Colonial Society of Massachusetts.
  http://www.colonialsociety.org/publications.html
Southern Association of Colleges and Schools
  http://www.sacscoc.org
Student Affairs Administrators in Higher Education
  www.naspa.org
United States Department of Education
  www.ed.gov/
Western Association of Schools and Colleges
  http://www.acswasc.org/about_overview.htm

Complete Glossary

Chapter 1

Pedagogy: instructional methods used in teaching

Carnegie Foundation for the Advancement of Teaching: founded by Andrew Carnegie in 1905 and serves as a policy and research center

Associate's degree: academic degree usually awarded after two years of study or the equivalent

For-profit: institutions that operate in order to generate a profit

Research institutions: institutions that conduct research as a primary mission

Master's level institutions: institutions that offer a baccalaureate and some master's degree programs

Baccalaureate: academic degree usually associated with a four-year undergraduate course of study

Chapter 2

New England: Northeast area of the United States; includes Maine, Vermont, Massachusetts, New Hampshire, Connecticut, and Rhode Island

Puritans: Christian religious group that left England seeking religious freedom

Colonial colleges: nine colleges founded during the colonial period

Disputation: formalized method of debate

Toleration: willingness to allow various Protestant religious denominations

Great Awakening: religious movement around the 1730s

Natural philosophy: study of nature and the physical universe

Syllogistic logic: formal analysis of logical terms and structures in order to infer the truth from a set of premises

Syllogistic disputation: formalized method of debate incorporating the use of syllogisms

Forensic disputation: formalized method of debate that allows ethical, emotional, and logical arguments

Natural history: study of plants and animals

Enlightenment: intellectual movement in Europe that promoted reason as a way to understand the universe and the human condition

Academies: postsecondary institutions that often taught liberal arts and practical skills to some degree

Phi Beta Kappa: founded in 1776, it is the nation's oldest honor society

Bad Butter Rebellion: one of the first student protests on record

John Adams: second president of the United States

Chapter 3

Civil War: war between the American states from 1861 to 1865

Liberal arts: originally included grammar, dialectic, rhetoric, arithmetic, geometry, music, and astronomy

Compulsory Education Law: law requiring school attendance, first passed in 1852 in Massachusetts

Preparatory departments: remedial instruction, offered in college, to prepare students for college-level studies

Legal precedent: legal principle, decided by a court, which provides authority that other courts may follow

Contract clause: Article 1, section 10, clause 1 of the U.S. Constitution prohibits states from enacting any law impairing the obligation of contracts

Normal school: designed to prepare teachers for the public school system

Coordinate college: single-sex college affiliated with a single-sex college of the opposite gender

American Missionary Association: integrated group of Protestant religious leaders who worked for the freedom and advancement of the Black population

Freedmen's Bureau: federal agency created after the Civil War to supervise relief and educational activities of freed slaves

Jesuit: Catholic priest who is a member of the Society of Jesus

Nonsectarian religion: Protestant religious orientation without regard to specific denomination

Lehrfreiheit: German, meaning freedom of the professor to investigate and teach the results of his/her research without governmental interference

Wissenschaft: German, meaning scholarly research and writing

Pure research: research for the value of discovery

Lernfreiheit: German, meaning freedom of the student to choose his/her own studies in an elective system

Applied research: research with the intention of solving a problem

Chapter 4

Great Depression: economic collapse that began in October 1929 and lasted about a decade

Comprehensive colleges: Post-secondary institutions that offer bachelor's and master's degree programs

Industrial education: programs designed specifically to prepare an individual for a vocation

Teaching-sisters: Catholic women religious who taught in Catholic schools

Wisconsin Idea: knowledge from colleges and universities should be used to solve real problems; higher education should be widely available and useful

Proprietary schools: schools that operate on a for-profit basis

Accreditation: process through which an institution demonstrates that it meets established standards

Carnegie Unit: standard period of study defining an academic course

Academic ranks: professorial ranks of instructor, assistant professor, associate professor, full professor

Academic freedom: freedom of the professor to investigate and teach/publish the results of his/her research without interference

Tenure: lifetime appointment granted after period of probationary service

Chapter 5

Civil Rights Act of 1964: outlawed segregation in businesses and banned discrimination in employment and public places

Civil Rights Movement: organized effort to secure civil rights, primarily through nonviolent means

Elementary and Secondary Education Act, 1965: legislated sweeping education reform aimed at elementary and secondary levels

Higher Education Act of 1965: focused on improving postsecondary education and provided significant financial aid for students

No Child Left Behind Act of 2001: reauthorization of the Elementary and Secondary Education Act intended to increase accountability and transparency

in loco parentis: refers to the tradition of faculty taking the role of parents in order to guide and discipline students

Family Education Rights and Privacy Act, 1974: protects the privacy of student education records

Student Nonviolent Coordinating Committee: one of the principal organizations supporting the Civil Rights Movement

Free Speech Movement: organized by students at the University of California at Berkeley to secure the right to freedom of speech on campus

Establishment: term used to describe the group holding social, political, and economic power and authority

Index

academic freedom, 104–110, 132
academies, 23, 29, 42–43, 50
accreditation, 53, 72, 74, 78–80, 84–90, 122–123, 132
Adams, John, 26, 61
African Methodist Episcopal Church, 46
Agassiz, Elizabeth Cary, 43
American Association of Junior Colleges, 83
American Association of Law Schools, 76
American Association of Teachers Colleges, 75
American Association of University Professors, 108–110, 132
American Bar Association, 76, 77
American Chemical Association, 66
American College Testing Service, 115
American Council on Education, 85, 88–89, 96–97
American Dental Association, 77
American Economic Association, 108

American Historical Association, 66
American Medical Association, 76–77
American Missionary Association, 46
American Philological Association, 66
American Political Science Association, 108
American Protective Association, 54
American Psychological Association, 66
American Revolution, 1, 13–15, 18–19, 21, 25, 31, 37, 40, 57, 61
American Sociological Association, 108
Annapolis, 92
Ashmun Institute, *see* Lincoln University
Association of American Colleges, 86, 108
Association of American Universities, 79, 86, 88
Association of Catholic Colleges, 79, 86
Association of Land-Grant Colleges, 86

athletics, 24, 67–68, 90–94, 114, 124
Atlanta University, 47
Avery College, 46

Bad Butter Rebellion, 25
Barnard College, 43
Bascom, John, 80
Bemis, Edward, 107
Berea College, 46
Brown University, 14, 18
Brown v. the Board of Education of Topeka, 101, 117
Brown, Francis, 31–34
Brown, J. Stanley, 82
Brown, Nicholas, 14
Bryn Mawr College, 43

Caldwell, Mary Gwendoline, 52
Cambridge University, 17–18
Capen, Samuel, 88–89
Carmichael, Stokely, 135
Carnegie, Andrew, 106
Carnegie Foundation for the Advancement of Teaching, 2, 4, 74, 76–77, 86–88, 92
Carroll, John, 52
Catholic Education Association, 87
Catholic institutions, 52–56, 77–80
Catholic University of America, 52–53, 79
Central State University, 46
Chauncey, Henry, 114
Cheyney University of Pennsylvania, 45–46
Civil Rights Act 1964, 117
Civil Rights Movement, 117, 133
Civil War, 28–30, 38, 40–41, 45–46, 51, 67, 73, 106
Clark, Jonas Gilman, 106
Clark University, 60
Clarke, Edward, 43–44
Cold War, 72
College and Academy of Philadelphia, *see* University of Pennsylvania
College Entrance Examination Board, 86, 114

College of New Jersey, *see* Princeton University
College of New Rochelle, 56
College of Notre Dame of Maryland, 55–56, 79
College of Rhode Island, *see* Brown University
College of St. Catherine, *see* St. Catherine University
College of St. Elizabeth, 56
College of William and Mary, 12, 16, 19, 22, 25
Collegiate School of Connecticut, *see* Yale University
Columbia University, 13, 18, 43, 68, 75, 136
common schools, 29
Commonwealth Fund, 106
community colleges, 81–84
compulsory education, 29–30, 46
Conant, James Bryant, 114
Congress of Racial Equality, 134
Cornell, Ezra, 106
Cornell University, 59, 64, 106, 113, 136
curriculum, 19–24, 29–30, 38–39, 42–44, 46–48, 53, 58, 61–62, 72–80, 83, 100, 129, 141

Dartmouth College, *see* Dartmouth University
Dartmouth College Case, 30–38
Dartmouth University, 15–18, 30–38,
Debating societies, *see* literary societies
Du Bois, W.E.B., 47–48
Dunster, Henry, 16, 20
Durant, Henry, 43
Durant, Pauline, 43

Educational Testing Service, 114
Eells, Walter, 83
Elementary and Secondary Education Act 1965, 119–120, 124
Eliot, Charles, 51
Ely, Richard, 107

Enlightenment, 23, 57, 105
enrollment, 6, 29, 44–45, 47–49, 63, 66, 73–76, 81–82, 84, 95–97, 99–102, 112–113, 125, 139–140

faculty, 6–7, 12, 19–20, 22–23, 58–60, 63–66, 78, 80, 88, 104–110, 131–133, 141
Family Educational Rights and Privacy Act 1974, 131
financial aid, student, 94–97, 101–104, 114, 120–124, 126–127, 129–131
Fisk University, 47
Flat Hat Club, 25
Flexner, Abraham, 77
Flexner Report, 77

Folwell, William Watts, 81
football, see athletics
Franklin, Benjamin, 14, 52
fraternities, 24, 67, 113–114
Free Speech Movement, 134–135
Freedmen's Bureau, 46–47

G.I. Bill of 1944, 95–97
General Education Board, 74, 86, 88, 106
Georgetown College, see Georgetown University
Georgetown University, 52
German influence, 59, 67, 105
Gilman, Daniel C., 60
Great Depression, 72, 94

Hall, G. Stanley, 60, 106
Hampton Institute, see Hampton University
Hampton University, 48, 74
Harper, William Rainey, 60, 81–82, 107
Harvard, John, 11, 15
Harvard, Statutes of, 11
Harvard Annex, 43
Harvard Charter of 1650, 18

Harvard College, see Harvard University
Harvard University, 9, 11, 13, 16, 18–19, 22, 24–25, 43, 47, 51, 58, 64, 66–68, 75, 91, 106, 114
Hasty Pudding Club, 25
Higher Education Act (1965), 120–122; (1972), 123; (1992), 123
Historically Black Colleges and Universities, 45–48, 74
Holmes, Henry W., 75
Howard University, 47, 114
Humphrey, Richard, 45

immigrants, 28, 53–54, 67, 80
Indian schools, 12, 13, 15–17
industrial education, 47–48, 74
Institute for Colored Youth, see Cheyney University of Pennsylvania

Jackson, Andrew, 58
Jackson State University, 136
Jefferson, Thomas, 22, 57, 61
Jesuits, 52, 77–79
Johns Hopkins University, 60, 64, 77, 106
Johnson, Lyndon B., 117, 119–120
Joliet Junior College, 82
Jordan, David Star, 108
junior colleges, see community colleges

Keane, John J., 60
Kennedy, John F., 117, 133
Kent State University, 136
Kerr, Clark, 135
King Jr., Martin Luther, 117
King's College, see Columbia University
Know-Nothing Party, 54
Koos, Leonard V., 82–83

Land Grant College Act, *see* Morrill Act

Lanham Act of 1940, 96

Lawrence, Abbott, 106

Legge, William, 15

Lehrfreiheit, 59, 105

Leland University, 47

Lernfreiheit, 59, 105

Leverett, John, 18

Lincoln, Abraham, 61

Lincoln University, 46, 47

literary societies, 24–25, 34–35, 67–67, 113

Lyon, Mary, 42–43

MacCracken, Henry M., 90

MacLean, John, 58

Manhattanville College, 79

Mann, Horace, 54

Meredith, James, 133–134

Modern Language Association, 66

Moor's Charity School, *see* Indian schools

Morrill, Justin Smith, 61–62

Morrill Act of 1862, 61–63; of 1890, 47, 63

Mount Holyoke College, 42–43

Mount Holyoke Female Seminary, *see* Mount Holyoke College

Mount St. Mary's College, 52

National Association of State Universities, 86

National Collegiate Athletic Association, 90–94

National Commission on Excellence in Education 1983, 124–129

National Defense Education Act 1958, 102–104, 121

National Merit Scholarship Program, 102

Native American Party, 54

native education (*see* Indian schools)

Nixon, Richard, 136

No Child Left Behind Act 2001, 124

normal schools, 42, 46–50, 74–75, 79

North Central Association of Colleges and Secondary Schools, 78–79, 85–86

Obama, Barack, 118

Oberlin College, 44, 46, 67

Occum, Samuel, 17

Oxford University, 17–18

Pembroke College, 14

Phi Beta Kappa, 25, 79

Pierce, Palmer E., 90–91

Pig Club, *see* Porcellian Club

Plain-Dealing Society, 25

Porcellian Club, 25

President's Commission on Higher Education 1947, 97–102

Princeton College, *see* Princeton University

Princeton University, 9, 13, 18, 21–22, 25, 58, 66, 68, 72, 92

professional education, 50–52, 76–77, 139

proprietary schools, 84, 139

Queens College, *see* Rutgers

Quincy, Josiah, 18

Radcliffe College, 43

Radcliffe Institute for Advanced Study at Harvard, 43

Ratio Studiorum, 78

Reid, William T., 91

Rensselaer Polytechnic Institute, 60

Rensselaer School, *see* Rensselaer Polytechnic Institute

Revolutionary War, *see* American Revolution

Rockefeller Sr., John D., 60, 65, 106

Roosevelt, Theodore, 90

Ross, Edward, 107–108

Rutgers, Colonel Henry, 15

Rutgers University, 14, 18, 68

Savio, Mario, 134
Scanlon, Marcella, 74
Scholastic Aptitude Test, 115
Scranton, William W., 137
Servicemen's Readjustment Act of 1944, *see* G.I. Bill of 1944
Seven Sisters Colleges, 43
Shaw University, 47
Silliman, Benjamin, 58
Smith, Sophia, 43
Smith, William, 14, 23
Smith College, 43
sororities, 113
Spellings, Margaret, 124
Sputnik, 72, 102
St. Catherine University, 79
St. Louis University, 77
St. Mary of the Woods College, 56
St. Mary's College (Baltimore), 52
St. Mary's College in South Bend (Notre Dame, Indiana), 56, 79
Stanford, Mrs. Leland, 107
Stanford University, 9, 64, 107
student life, 24–26, 66–68, 111–114, 137–138, 141
Student Nonviolent Coordinating Committee, 133–135
Students for a Democratic Society, 134

Tappan, Henry, 81
Taylor, Joseph, 43
Teachers College of Columbia University, *see* Columbia University
Teachers Insurance and Annuity Association, 87
Thomas, M. Carey, 43
Trinity College, 56, 79
Truman, Harry, 97
Trustees of Dartmouth College v. Woodward, 30–38
Tuskegee Institute, *see* Tuskegee University
Tuskegee University, 48, 74
tutor, *see* faculty

United States Naval Academy, *see* Annapolis
University of California Berkeley, 134
University of Chicago, 60, 64, 81–82, 89, 106–107
University of Georgia, 56
University of Massachusetts at Amherst, 66–67
University of Michigan, 81, 84
University of Minnesota, 81
University of North Carolina, 56
University of Notre Dame, 79
University of Pennsylvania, 14, 18, 23, 25
University of Phoenix, 5, 132
University of Virginia, 45, 57, 67, 93
University of Wisconsin, 80, 107, 136

Van Hise, Charles, 80
Van Rensselaer, Stephen, 60
Vassar, Matthew, 43
Vassar College, 42–44
Veteran's Readjustment Assistance Act 1952, 90
Vietnam War, 117, 133, 135, 137–138
vocational colleges, *see* community colleges

War of 1812, 27–28
Washington, Booker T., 48
Webster, Daniel, 35
Wellesley College, 42–43
Well-Meaning Club, 25
West Point Academy, 61, 90
Wheelock, Eleazar, 15, 17
Wheelock, John, 18, 30-34
White, Andrew D., 106
Wilberforce University, 46–47
Wilson, Woodrow, 13
Wisconsin Idea, 80
Wissenschaft, 59
Wolff, Madeleva, 79
women's education, 23–24, 40–45, 55–56, 73–76, 79–80
Women's Rights Convention 1848, 41
Woodward, William, 30–36

Works, George A., 89
World War I, 71–72, 74, 85
World War II, 72, 84, 94, 97–98

Yale, Elihu, 13, 15
Yale College, *see* Yale University
Yale Report of 1828, 38–39
Yale University, 9, 13, 18, 22, 24–25,
    38–39, 58, 64, 67–68, 92

Zook, George, 97

Peter Lang
PRIMERS
in Education

Peter Lang Primers are designed to provide a brief and concise introduction or supplement to specific topics in education. Although sophisticated in content, these primers are written in an accessible style, making them perfect for undergraduate and graduate classroom use. Each volume includes a glossary of key terms and a References and Resources section.

Other published and forthcoming volumes cover such topics as:

- Standards
- Popular Culture
- Critical Pedagogy
- Literacy
- Higher Education
- John Dewey
- Feminist Theory and Education

- Studying Urban Youth Culture
- Multiculturalism through Postformalism
- Creative Problem Solving
- Teaching the Holocaust
- Piaget and Education
- Deleuze and Education
- Foucault and Education

Look for more Peter Lang Primers to be published soon. To order other volumes, please contact our Customer Service Department:

      800-770-LANG (within the US)
      212-647-7706 (outside the US)
      212-647-7707 (fax)

To find out more about this and other Peter Lang book series, or to browse a full list of education titles, please visit our website:

www.peterlang.com